No Magic Formula

LeRoy Eims

NAVPRESS

A MINISTRY OF THE NAVIGATORS

P.O. Box 20, Colorado Springs, Colorado 80901

*Unless otherwise noted, Scripture
quotations from the Old Testament are
from the* New American Standard Bible
(NASB), © *The Lockman Foundation
1960, 1962, 1963, 1968, 1971, 1972, 1973,
1975, and are used by permission. All New
Testament quotations are from the* New
International Version:New Testament,
Copyright © *New York International Bible
Society, 1973, Used by Permission. Other
versions used are the* King James Version
(KJV); *J.B. Phillips:* The New Testament
in Modern English, Revised Edition (PH),
©*J.B. Phillips 1958, 1960, 1972; the*
Amplified New Testament (AMP), © *The
Lockman Foundation 1954, 1958, and
used by permission; and from* The New
English Bible (NEB), © *The Delegates of
the Oxford University Press and The
Syndics of the Cambridge University Press
1961, 1970. Reprinted by permission.*

*The Navigators is an international,
interdenominational Christian
organization. Jesus Christ gave His
followers a Great Commission in Matthew
28:19, "Therefore go and make disciples
of all nations . . ." The primary aim
of The Navigators is to help fulfill that
commission by making disciples and
developing disciplemakers in every nation.*

Printed in the United States of America

CONTENTS

To the memory of
PAUL LITTLE
who through the triumph of Jesus Christ
has gained the ultimate victory

FOREWORD

As I read this book, it occurred to me that the volume is as timely as any being published today, and I have been reading some relevant books on hunger, the poor, church institutionalism and growth, and many others. This book is for NOW precisely because of its timeliness—its Old Testamentness and its emphasis on the Jewishness of our faith.

For the past few years as a pastor I have been sensing a certain deep lack among conservative evangelicals. I have found that good biblical words, such as *believe, faith, disciple,* and others, have somehow lost their meaning. The awareness and awesomeness of divine sovereignty seems to be missing in daily life and practice. The words were there, but somehow they were empty. Christian faith and life were somehow shallow, superficial, horizontal, thin, academic, cerebral, and doctrinaire. Growing emphasis has been on the *how* of everything and the how seemed reduced to the mechanical, the technique; almost the gimmick. Missing has been the dynamic. Christian faith and life seem to have capitulated to our technological culture to be shaped in the mold of Madison Avenue, TV commercials, and solutions. Profound truth has been reduced to instant answers; missing has been the vertical, the visceral, the nourishing.

Out of these observations has gradually emerged the realization that we had lost at least to some degree the Jewishness of our faith. We had divorced the New Testament from the Old; we had abandoned our legacy—the wisdom of the ages—given to us by the ancient people of God—our ancestors in the faith. So I began taking the Old Testament seriously as never before, and the result has been revolutionary in my thought, life, and teaching.

Now comes this exciting, practical volume by one whose every approach to faith is down to earth—"where the rubber meets the road." LeRoy Eims is a student of the Word in the fullest sense. His work reflects careful, inductive study of the Bible. Free from cliches, it bristles with fresh, imaginative, original, born-of-careful observation study of Scripture.

We are in a warfare and no generation of Christians has faced greater, albeit the strategy of the enemy in our day is more sophisticated and subtle. The experiences and exploits of our ancestors in the faith were recorded for our edification and living. LeRoy Eims has given the people of God a guide and model for personal and collective triumph in an age when secularism, materialism, and faithlessness are bent on destroying the Church and all it stands for.

This book restores us to wholeness of personhood. It is impossible to compartmentalize our faith, isolating it from the rest of life, if we take the instruction and exhortation of this book seriously. The book is authored by one who, with his brothers and sisters in The Navigators, studies the Bible, not simply to know the Bible better, but to know how it relates to life and what it requires of him. With him, doctrine is an order to duty; belief is an order to practice; and this book will help the believer on such a pilgrimage.

Richard C. Halverson
Fourth Presbyterian Church
Washington, D.C.

PREFACE

I hate war and everything connected with it. The horror of watching a close friend blown to bits. The agony of aching muscles, a parched tongue, blistered feet, days and nights without sleep. The terror of hitting a beach amidst machine gun bullets, mortar fire, land mines, and artillery shells. As a young marine in World War II these things were a reality. I didn't want to; I didn't like it; but I had to face them.

As a Christian, I now have the same reaction to the spiritual battles of life. I prefer smooth sailing, but storms arise. I prefer life without troubles, but difficulties come. It is evident as we read our Bibles that we, the people of God, are at war. We're in a conflict. The New Testament, for example, crackles with military talk. The Ephesians were alerted to get their armor on. Timothy was charged to fight the good fight of faith and endure hardness as a good soldier of Jesus Christ. James and Paul spoke of striving in fervent prayer. Faith was a shield to quench the fiery darts of the devil. The Word of God was called a sword. Paul was not shadowboxing; he was in a real fight with a real enemy.

The Old Testament is a clear picture of all this. The preparation for battle and the wars of the people of God are all lessons for us, graphic illustrations of the way our unchangeable God works today. Through the Old Testament you can relive the ancient past of your spiritual ancestors and learn lessons vital to your spiritual life today.

Spiritual victory is the heritage of the child of God. Jesus came to destroy the works of the devil. As His followers we are on the winning team.

This book goes forth to all of my comrades-in-arms engaged in the spiritual warfare of life with the earnest prayer that it will be used by the Lord to provide instruction, encouragement, and inspiration we all need to stand against the enemy of our souls.

CHAPTER ONE

SPIRITUAL VICTORY CAN BE YOURS

Study Material: Exodus 12:29—15:27; Deuteronomy 8:2-3;
Romans 15:4; 1 Corinthians 10:11; 2 Corinthians 10:4;
Ephesians 6:10-20; Colossians 2:15; 2 Timothy 2:3

S PIRITUAL victory is the promised possession of every
believer, provided that the Christian has a vital relationship with Jesus Christ and that he goes about obtain-
ing victory God's way. It is not something reserved only
for spiritual superstars. Every Christian can have victory
in the continual spiritual battles in which he is engaged.

Battles come and battles go. In all shapes and sizes.
Some are easily won; some are mean, ugly, tough. While I
was serving with the Marines in World War II, this point
was driven home to me quite vividly. Sometimes the
fighting was unbelievably fierce and casualties ran high.
Then things would loosen up a bit and the outfit would
have a breathing spell—a chance to catch some sleep or at
least get something to eat.

Spiritual warfare is like that. Our enemy never quits,
but there are times when the intensity of the battle di-
minishes. We get a chance to catch our breath, relax,
regain perspective, and feed on the Word of God.

As a new Marine recruit, I was fascinated by old salts
spinning their yarns. They would tell about their days in
Nicaragua and the times they served with Chesty or Red
Mike. The Old China Marines would talk about the way it

used to be—the Old Corps—and look at us new boots with a combination of disdain and pity.

I experienced the same sort of thing as a new Christian in college. Old warriors of the Cross, who had served the Lord in Africa or China, would speak in chapel. They would tell of the faithfulness of God down through the years. I would sit spellbound as they told of working under unbelievable hardships, and then made such statements as: "In 50 years of serving the Lord, He never failed me one single time." My spirit would tremble and my heart beat with wild excitement as I yearned to go forth and plunge into the conflicts that would affect eternity.

Spiritual battles are fought on many battlegrounds. You can generally tell where a person is fighting by the sort of problems he has.

When our Marine company hit the beach at Peleliu, our problems were of a "front line" nature. Ammunition was in short supply. Communications were unreliable. A man fighting near me had his left arm blown off. Land mines were disabling many of our tanks and jeeps. Water was scarce. We had to go without sleep.

Before the invasion, however, our outfit was stationed on a small island hundreds of miles from the battle zone. Was everything lovely there? Hardly. We had constant problems, but of a different sort than at Peleliu. Our tents leaked; one guy kept the rest of us awake nights with his snoring; it rained halfway through the outdoor movie. Occasionally we would find land crabs in our shoes. The blowflies, mosquitos, and red ants were a nuisance. Too often there were no letters at mail call. The coffee was too weak or too strong.

In the spiritual realm, too, battles are fought on the front line and in the rest areas. One person is concerned about his neighbor's salvation while another is upset with the color of the baby blankets in the church nursery. One person can't stand the way his fellow committee member wears his necktie while another is in prayer all night for his sick child. One is about to leave the church over a personality conflict with the church soloist while another is laboring night and day to make sure the missions budget is met. Battles. All shapes and sizes. "Front line" and "rest area." Some concerned with advancing the kingdom of God—others with secondary issues or self.

This book concerns spiritual warfare, and our backdrop is the great lessons God taught the Israelites as He brought them out of Egypt and took them into the Promised Land. We will look at the years of preparation in the wilderness, the battles of Canaan, and the lessons God taught in relation to victory in those battles. We will see that throughout these situations, there was no magic formula, no one way in which God taught and led and gave victory to His people.

WHY STUDY THE OLD TESTAMENT?

In a fascinating passage which gives great insight into the Old Testament, Paul states, "These things happened to them as examples and were written down as warnings for us, on whom the fulfillment of the ages has come" (1 Corinthians 10:11). Did you get that? *What happened to the people of Israel was intended as lessons for us, who live in the present age.*

The Apostle Paul also said, "For everything that was written in the past was written to teach us, so that through endurance and the encouragement of the Scriptures we might have hope" (Romans 15:4). Here again we are brought face to face with the vital ministry of the Old

Testament to our daily lives. Its pages are alive with precepts and examples to guide us.

When you grasp this concept, the Old Testament springs to life. You see yourself time and time again. As you read about the Israelites' flight from the Egyptians who are coming up hard behind them, bent on destruction, you can put yourself into the scene. What would you do? You can't go either to the left or to the right, the sea is before you, and the chariots, spears, and trained soldiers of the Egyptian army are behind.

You might see yourself at the fortress city of Jericho. As you stand with those unassailable walls in front of you, what do you do? Imagine yourself also with Israel in the middle of a parched wilderness—no water anywhere around. How will you survive?

We will learn from the Old Testament how God gave Israel victory. Sometimes we will see why the Israelites tasted defeat. And in it all, we will discover truths for our own spiritual conflicts and victories.

WHY TALK OF WARFARE AND VICTORY?

The warfare theme runs in a grand sweep through the entire Bible. An ages-long conflict rages between the kingdom of God and the kingdom of Satan. Heaven and hell never declare a truce. Light and darkness will never mesh. Satan and Christ can never come to terms.

The first biblical prophecy about Jesus Christ is in the context of spiritual warfare. God promised that although the heel of the Seed (Christ) should be bruised, the final victory would be His. He would bruise the serpent's head and win the war (see Genesis 3:15). Meanwhile, what state is to prevail? *Enmity. Conflict. Warfare.*

By His death on the cross, Christ dealt a fatal blow to the devil's kingdom. "And having disarmed the powers and authorities, He made a public spectacle of them, triumphing over them by the cross" (Colossians 2:15). Now, though the battle still rages, the tide of battle has turned and one day Satan's overthrow will be complete.

Believers in New Testament times saw the Christian life as a warfare. Paul, for example, exhorted the Ephesians in military terms. "Finally, be strong in the Lord and in His mighty power. Put on the full armor of God so that you can take your stand against the devil's schemes. For our struggle is not against flesh and blood, but against the rulers, against the authorities, against the powers of this dark world and against the spiritual forces of evil in the heavenly realms" (Ephesians 6:10-12). He also reminded the Corinthians that the weapons of their warfare were not carnal, but mighty through God (see 2 Corinthians 10:4).

What was true in Paul's day is true now, and the battles of the Old Testament provide abundant illustrations of the conflict between the purposes of God and those of Satan. From Genesis to Revelation, conflict between right and wrong, good and evil, darkness and light abounds.

GOD PREPARES HIS PEOPLE FOR VICTORY

Let's observe in a preliminary way how God dealt with His people after saving them from Egyptian bondage. "Now it came about when Pharaoh had let the people go, that God did not lead them by the way of the land of the Philistines, even though it was near; for God said, 'Lest the people change their minds when they see war, and they return to Egypt.' Hence God led the people around by the way of the wilderness to the Red Sea; and the sons of Israel went up in martial array from the land of Egypt" (Exodus 13:17-18).

The first thing to notice here is that *God led them.* Moses gave the directions, but God was the leader. Although at times along the way the people doubted that fact, God *was* in control. He sent them on their journey. He made the choice as to the way they should go. He was their guide.

Permeating Scripture is the basic promise that God leads His people. The assurance of guidance is as basic in the Bible as is the assurance of victory. God is well able, ready, and eager to give us the guidance we need. "For this God is our God forever and ever; He will be our guide even unto death" (Psalm 48:14, KJV).

The Lord not only shows us the way; He goes forth to lead us in it. "When He has brought out all His own, He goes on ahead of them, and His sheep follow Him because they know His voice" (John 10:4). Christ is the Good Shepherd and we are the sheep of His pasture. As we follow Him who knows the end from the beginning, we can rest in the assurance that because of His great love for us He can be trusted to lead us into the best paths.

"Thus says the Lord, your Redeemer, the Holy One of Israel, 'I am the Lord your God, who teaches you to profit, who leads you in the way you should go' " (Isaiah 48:17). As teacher and guide, He enlightens our eyes and directs our steps. And the longer we follow Him, the more confident we become of His wisdom, power, and goodness.

By what means does God actually lead us? Scripture says, "The mind of man plans his way, but the Lord directs his steps" (Proverbs 16:9). Dawson Trotman, founder of The Navigators, used to say that God gave us a great amount of leading when He gave us a mind. As rational beings, we have the ability to think and plan. We can set goals and can devise ways and means to reach them. But we must do it all within the framework of the glory of God. When we do that, we can rest in the delightful confidence that God will not let us stray out of bounds. "In all thy ways acknowledge Him, and He shall direct thy paths" (Proverbs 3:6, KJV). At times God's ways will not be what we intended or what seems right at the time. But never mind. When our eyes are on God, He will not only direct in the great affairs of life, but will lead in every step we take.

Two routes led from Egypt to Canaan. One was a shortcut, less than a week's journey. The other, much longer, led through the wilderness. God took His people the long way. Why? "And you shall remember all the way which the Lord your God has led you in the wilderness these forty years, *that He might humble you, testing you, to know what was in your heart, whether you would keep His commandments or not.* And He humbled you and let you be hungry, and fed you with manna which you did not know, nor did your fathers know, *that He might make you understand that man does not live by bread alone, but man lives by everything that proceeds out of the mouth of the Lord"* (Deuteronomy 8:2-3).

The wilderness became the Israelites' school, their training ground, their boot camp. They were soon to put it all to work—to apply the lessons of the desert to the battles in the Promised Land.

The same principle applies to us today. By God's love and grace, we are led through experiences in life that can encourage and train us to serve Him better and trust Him more fully in the days ahead.

From time to time the Israelites were brought to the brink of disaster, only to learn that it was their own pride that took them there. Through such experiences, God humbled them. He gave them a good look at themselves and taught them to rely on Him.

Time and again He also tested their obedience in that desert proving ground, and their inner motives were revealed. As we read of Israel's experiences, we begin to realize that spiritual training is far more demanding than military training. There are many good soldiers but few real men of God. Hammering hardens steel but crumbles putty. God is out to make us good soldiers.

As soon as we enlist in the army of God, as disciples of Jesus Christ, our stress training begins. Though it is tough, a paradox emerges. In the midst of training and testing, we find songs of joy and praise. Peace reigns supreme in our hearts and boundless excitement pounds in our breasts as we realize we are being swept along in the eternal purposes of God and have found that for which we were created.

In Egypt, the people of Israel were in sad shape —oppressed slaves without hope. They were totally ignorant of the things of God; they were quarrelsome and addicted to the idols of Egypt. God could not take such people directly from Egypt to Canaan. He needed time to prepare them to be a people He could use to bless and teach all the world. Patiently He taught them, giving them commandments as they were able to receive them.

The psalmist said, "And He led them forth by the right way, that they might go to a city of habitation" (Psalm 107:7, KJV). God's way is the right way, though at times it may appear to be the long way, the hard way, or the wrong way. God knows what He's doing and always has our best interest at heart. We can count on that.

Scripture says that God led Israel through the wilderness because the people were not ready for war. Their spirits had been broken by slavery; they could not effectively turn from a bricklayer's trowel to a sword overnight. The mean, tough Canaanites were far too strong for these raw recruits.

It's a blessing to realize that God knows our frame. He remembers that we are dust. He takes us through smaller trials first, so that we will be able to handle the big battles ahead. Often God takes us through a wilderness, but He will not leave us there. That is a tremendous blessing. We have the assurance in trials that God will lead us through to the other side.

How sure can we be that God will see us through? Well, how did He treat Israel? "Even when they made for themselves a calf of molten metal and said, 'This is your God who brought you up from Egypt,' and committed great blasphemies, Thou in Thy great compassion, didst not forsake them in the wilderness" (Nehemiah 9:18-19). God stuck by Israel despite its great sin, and He'll surely stick by us.

THE NECESSITY OF TRIALS

Now let's start our journey. We'll begin with the children of Israel, fresh out of Egypt, facing the Red Sea. They can't go to the left or to the right. "And as Pharaoh drew near, the sons of Israel looked, and behold, the Egyptians were marching after them, and they became very frightened; so the sons of Israel cried out to the Lord" (Exodus 14:10).

Note that Israel had two sources of distress here. First, "the Egyptians were marching after them." They had opposition from outside. Second, "they became very frightened." They had fear within.

The Christian is constantly caught in this sort of deadly cross fire. The Apostle Paul, describing his own experience, wrote, "Without were fightings, within were fears" (2 Corinthians 7:5, KJV). Outside the Body of Christ were the avowed enemies of the Cross and the wolves in sheep's clothing—false apostles and workers who masqueraded as ministers of righteousness while they promoted error and undermined the truth. They tried to have Paul thrown in jail or killed and constantly promoted lies about him. While this battle raged hot and heavy, the battle within went on and on as well. Paul speaks of fears. He was troubled, perplexed, cast down.

As we read of this kind of dilemma, we can identify with the problem. There are always outside threats with which we have to cope. Financial burdens grow heavier. Our personal generation gap grows wider as children and parents are at odds. Sickness strikes, bringing pain, grief, and devastating hospital costs. Our church has pressing needs. The Sunday School cries for attention.

In addition to all the problems from outside, there are problems within that are hard to face. The corruption of our own flesh plagues us. We recognize the truth of the words of Jesus: "The spirit is willing, but the body is weak" (Matthew 26:41). When people misunderstand us, we ache with disappointment. Our hearts become heavy, our minds try to cope, and our spirits lag. The war is on, and the battle is very real. When we read in the Bible that man is born to trouble, we nod in agreement. Our experience tells us it is so.

The children of Israel, finding themselves in such a situation, began to complain. "They said to Moses, 'Is it because there were no graves in Egypt that you have taken us away to die in the wilderness? Why have you dealt with us in this way, bringing us out of Egypt? Is this not the word that we spoke to you in Egypt, saying, "Leave us alone that we may serve the Egyptians"? For it would have been better for us to serve the Egyptians than to die in the wilderness' " (Exodus 14:11-12).

One of the greatest blessings ever given to a people was theirs. They had just been delivered from the cruelest of bondage and already were complaining. The same pattern is true today. Whenever we are given a liberty, we will generally encounter some difficulty.

Note Moses' reply. He did not bristle in anger, but tried to comfort the people. "Do not fear! Stand by and see the salvation of the Lord which He will accomplish for you today; for the Egyptians whom you have seen today, you will never see them again forever. The Lord will fight for you while you keep silent" (14:13-14).

Then a strange and wonderful thing happened. "And the angel of God, who had been going before the camp of Israel, moved and went behind them; and the pillar of cloud moved from before them and stood behind them. So it came between the camp of Egypt and the camp of Israel; and there was the cloud along with the darkness, yet it gave light at night. Thus the one did not come near the other all night" (14:19-20).

At this point the Israelites didn't need guidance; they needed God's immediate protection. The pillar, which had been their guide, changed position and separated them from the armies of Egypt. We should learn an important lesson here. Whatever we need, God provides. And His timing is perfect, even though it may sometimes appear a little late to us. We all know the story's end. God delivered His people and destroyed the enemy. But will we remember that the next time we are in a corner?

The Hebrew young men in the fiery furnace had no way out. But they were delivered. Daniel's road to the lion's den was supposed to be a one-way street, but he came back. Peter, watched in prison by 16 guards, was to be killed at dawn. But while the guards slept, the doors flew open and he walked out.

All too often we give up too soon. Right now you may be in a situation that *appears* hopeless, caught between an Egyptian army and a Red Sea. Stand still and see God's salvation. Set your confidence in Him. "So we say with confidence, 'The Lord is my helper; I will not be afraid. What can man do to me?'" (Hebrews 13:6)

The first thing the Israelites did after their deliverance from the enemy was to praise God. They sang of what He had done and of what He surely would do. Their hearts were full of faith, thanksgiving, and praise. Then they came to the waters of Marah and found them bitter. When we meet such disappointments and troubles, we can either trust God or complain. Israel complained.

That's deadly. Complaining can lead to bitterness, which has powerful destructive effects. When a person is bitter, he is likely to spread his disease to others. If he is angry at someone, he will often try to run down the person to others, thus spreading his bitterness. But the most destructive effect of bitterness is on the person himself. A bitter substance fouls the container that holds it.

When I was in grade school, I went to a Boy Scout camp. Each of us was to bring a can of fruit or vegetables and the camp would supply the rest. Since our family was extremely poor, the county would give us "relief baskets" containing canned goods, but there was a hitch. All the labels were removed so you never knew what you were getting. So I left for camp with an unlabeled can. When I opened it, I was surprised to find unsweetened grapefruit juice, and I drank a cup or two of it. Then it was announced that we could come to the fire and get some hot chocolate. I was elated. We never had hot chocolate at home, for it was too expensive. So I ran forward, filled my cup, and took a sip. I couldn't believe it. My chance had come to have hot chocolate and it tasted awful. The reason? The little bit of unsweetened grapefruit juice in my cup had spoiled the taste. I poured out my chocolate, washed out my cup, and went back to the fire for more. No deal. The rule was only one cup per boy.

Complaining not only spreads bitterness; it can also stunt our spiritual growth. To grow, we must both feed and nourish our souls on God's Word, and respond in faith to *disappointments and trials*. Then our trials draw us closer to God. Otherwise the devil uses them to drive a wedge between us and the Lord and to destroy our fellowship. And a person out of fellowship with God is not growing.

In a difficult situation similar to Israel's thirst at Marah, David drew closer to God. "O God, Thou art my God; I shall seek Thee earnestly; my soul thirsts for Thee, my flesh yearns for Thee, in a dry and weary land where there is no water" (Psalm 63:1).

Difficult times that are bitter to our souls put our belief in the loving sovereignty of God to the test. They reveal our basic attitudes toward His perfect control. If we see His hand in everything, our complaints will be replaced with settled trust.

Here's a word of encouragement for us: Do you know what lay beyond the bitter waters of Marah? The sweet waters of Elim. "Then they came to Elim where there were twelve springs of water and seventy date palms, and they camped there beside the waters" (Exodus 15:27).

Each of us tastes the bitter waters of life at one time or

another. If you haven't come to the waters of Marah as yet, you will. No one is exempt. Some Christians falsely believe it is a mark of failure or unspiritual behavior to admit a problem exists. They assume that Christians should go through life free of the world's difficulties and tears.

I once spoke to a group from a Christian organization, and the director announced that I would be available for counseling afterward. Everyone who came began the conversation by saying, "I have not come because I have a problem." Then that person would proceed to tell me about all kinds of problems and we would look into the Word of God together and have prayer.

The idea that Christians are exempt from everyday difficulties is nonsense. It is also unscriptural. Jesus said, "I have told you these things, so that in Me you may have peace. In this world you will have trouble. But take heart! I have overcome the world" (John 16:33).

It has been my experience that the tough times of life can lead us into closer and sweeter fellowship with God and greater fruitfulness in His service. Men and women of God are fashioned on the anvil of affliction. The pressures of life can be used of the Holy Spirit to mold us more and more into the image of Christ. Greater usefulness, more abundant fruitfulness, deeper fellowship, and a more Christlike character can result as the Lord leads us through the bitter waters of life. Everything depends on our responses. If we curse God for bringing us to the waters of Marah, chances are we will never come to the sweet waters and fruitful palms of Elim.

If today you are standing by the waters of Marah, ask God for grace to praise and thank Him for His goodness. It's tough to do. But there's no use hiding your head in the sand and pretending the trouble is not there. Paul said,

"While we are in this tent, we groan and are burdened" (2 Corinthians 5:4). Though the calamities of life are a heavy load, God uses them for His own great purposes.

TO BECOME MORE THAN CONQUERORS

God's training of the Israelites in the wilderness is a fascinating study. It was God's way of preparing them for the future wars of Canaan, and He needed 40 years to discipline His people. But it transformed them from a nation of slaves—weakened in spirit and crushed in will by two centuries of slavery—into a nation of conquerors (see the Book of Joshua).

When we receive Christ, we are delivered from years of slavery to sin. God takes our lives and transforms us into a people who are more than conquerors through Jesus Christ (see Romans 8:35-39). This is God's plan for every one of us.

If you had set out to design a training program to prepare the Israelites for the wars of Canaan, what would you have done? Two centuries of slavery had distorted their personalities. Complaining had become their way of life. Every day they faced a hard and hopeless outlook. They knew the torment of the tyrant's whip. Weariness, hunger, and pain met them with every sunrise. They were a defeated, hopeless, cantankerous lot. They *trusted* nobody.

When Moses returned to help them, they assumed he really didn't have their interests at heart. They had learned to watch out for nobody but number one. They had taken on the idolatry of Egypt which—ingrained in their souls—appealed to their sensual natures and fed their lusts. They had become deeply infected by the foul, depraved, immoral way of life that is always a part of heathen religion.

At work they tried to do as little as possible. When an order was given, they schemed and connived to get around it. If they could slide by and survive, they had gained the day. The rods, whips, and cruelty of their taskmasters killed their courage. They bowed and scraped before the Egyptians. I have seen the effects of government by dictators, whose means of rule are fear and death to all who resist. I have seen the lifeless eyes, sloped shoulders, and shuffled walk of such people.

God intended to transform these people into a nation of conquerors despite almost unbelievable odds. They were to raise the flag of victory and ride the highway of success, singing His praises. God would use them greatly in the centuries ahead.

Admittedly He couldn't have chosen a more unlikely people. But then, God's ways are not ours. He can bring much from little. He can bring joy out of sorrow, victory out of defeat. Every hour of every day all over the world, He guides men and women—from every nation, from every situation in life, from every religious background, or no background—who place their faith in the Lord Jesus Christ and enter His school to be trained by Him for usefulness in His kingdom.

So the Israelites began their grand adventure with God. What would He teach them? How would He accomplish His objectives? Our pursuit of those answers will lead us into an exciting and personally rewarding study. The truths of God should burst on our senses as we see vivid lessons for our own lives, and embark on new paths of victory, devotion, and service.

One tremendous lesson overshadows all the rest —there is no magic formula for victory in Christ. We cannot learn one simple strategy and then rest on that for the duration of the war. Our creative God loves variety. At one point He will lead us by one way, and just as we get comfortable and complacent in that, He will seemingly change His direction and lead us by another unmarked trail. His purpose, of course, is to teach us something new and valuable for growth in our Christian lives and service for Him.

I can see and hear Dawson Trotman, founder of The Navigators, to this day. He would gather us in his living room or at a conference grounds and drive home the point as only he could do it, "Gang, there is no magic formula. And if you think there is, you've just lost it."

Then he would launch into a story to illustrate the point. One of his favorites grew out of the Billy Graham campaign in Chattanooga. Daws had taken a few fledgling Navigators with him to help in the ministry. They set up chairs, distributed follow-up materials, and ran errands. After the campaign, one of them was invited to serve in the next one. Daws, in his usual fashion, looked over the new city, the new stadium, the new circumstances, and began to devise a new program to fit the situation. The young Navigator watched him and one day made the near-fatal mistake. As Daws was busily building a new follow-up procedure to fit the new mission, the young man said, "Daws, why are you doing it that way? That's not the way we did it in Chattanooga."

Remember. However much you've already learned, there's more. However much success you have achieved, there's probably a better way. Wisdom did not die in Chattanooga. Nor have you yet reached perfection in your Christian growth and service.

That's one of the truths that will become evident as you follow the children of Israel across the sands of the great desert. At various points along the way, God will drive home a lesson. It will be unexpected and different. But it will get the point across and change the lives of the people involved. As we go with Israel from one lesson to the next, let us be alert for truth that can be applied to our own lives by the power of the Holy Spirit. Life is full of bends and turns in the road. As we follow our Leader and Guide, we'll see many truths vividly, but we'll learn *no magic formula*.

TOPICS FOR STUDY

1. How did the Israelites get to Egypt in the first place? Why did God send them there? (Genesis 37—50)
2. What procedure did God follow to get His people out of Egypt? (Exodus 1—12)
3. The importance of leadership.
4. The principle of no victory without a battle.
5. God's promise of victory (Romans 8).
6. The battles of the Christian and his protection (Ephesians 6:10-20).

APPLICATION: How can I apply the teachings of this chapter to my own life? Write out some specific things that you can do.

PART ONE

BASIC TRAINING

Israel's Preparation in the Wilderness

CHAPTER TWO

HERE'S YOUR SHIELD
The Lesson of Faith

Study Material: Exodus 16–17; Isaiah 40–41; Daniel 2; John 7; Acts 16; 1 Corinthians 10

THE first lesson the children of Israel had to learn in preparation for their entry into the Promised Land was the lesson of faith. Obviously. For the next 40 years, it would be just them and God. He had the road map. He had the food. He alone could keep them in shoes and clothing. So off they went into the unknown testings of the bleak wilderness. As we sit surrounded by comforts and luxuries, we may well look back at them with a mixture of sadness and pity. *Imagine!* we might think, *all they had was God.* As it turned out, He was all they needed.

One hard, biting winter in 18th century Scotland, during a severe famine, a small, frail, elderly woman entered a store clutching a few coppers. She bought a penny's worth of this and a penny's worth of that. When she was down to her last penny, she said, "With this one I'll buy oil for my lamp so that I can read my Bible. 'Tis my only source of comfort during the cold, long winter night."

As we picture her frail, bent figure, we may feel a sense of sadness and pity. *What a shame!* we may think. But is she to be pitied? Admittedly her only solace was the Word of God. Yes, she was cold and hungry. But she is not cold or hungry today; she sits at the feet of her Lord, filled with the wonder of His presence. During her earthly life, all she had was God. As it turned out, He was all she needed.

There is a tremendous lesson in this for us. What do we really need besides God? Will He not provide for us, comfort us, guide us, teach us, and strengthen us? Perhaps one of our 20th century problems is that we have learned to rely on God plus, with the emphasis on the plus. Not so with the Hebrew people who headed for Canaan. God was their all. As they began their journey, they hardly knew Him. Could He be believed? Could He be trusted? That issue had to be dealt with at once. Many lessons were necessary and important, but this one was crucial. Since their trust in God was the key to the whole enterprise, the Lord began by teaching them the lesson of faith.

TRUSTING FOR DAILY NEEDS

Many of us have joyfully trusted Jesus Christ for salvation, and we now rest confidently in His ability to save and keep us through eternity. We rest in the promise of Scripture: "God has given us eternal life, and this life is in His Son. He who has the Son has life; he who does not have the Son of God does not have life" (1 John 5:11-12).

Paradoxically, many of us trust God for eternity but doubt His power in our daily lives. Scientists tell us a human body is worth perhaps $20 on the open market. But what is a soul worth? Jesus said it was worth more than all the wealth in the world. A soul lives throughout eternity. A physical body on the average will last about 70 years. We entrust an eternal soul to Jesus—worth more than the combined wealth of the world—and hesitate to trust Him with a passing $20 body.

Can we trust God for our needs as they arise day by day?

This was the issue with which God began Israel's training. "Then they set out from Elim, and all the congregation of the sons of Israel came to the wilderness of Sin, which is between Elim and Sinai, on the fifteenth day of the second month after their departure from the land of Egypt. And the whole congregation of the sons of Israel grumbled against Moses and Aaron in the wilderness. And the sons of Israel said to them, 'Would that we had died by the Lord's hand in the land of Egypt, when we sat by the pots of meat, when we ate bread to the full; for you have brought us out into this wilderness to kill this whole assembly with hunger' " (Exodus 16:1-3).

The Israelites had been out of Egypt only a month and a half. The text suggests that there was some discussion among them as to whether God or Moses had brought them out. So they complained to Moses and Aaron, "You have brought us out into this wilderness" (16:3).

We often respond similarly. When the going gets rough, we question whether the Lord is in the situation or not. Our daughter, Becky, and her husband, Rich, became convinced that the Lord wanted them to move to Colorado where they could get further training and help in their spiritual growth and ministry. Rich came out and, during his first day in town, found a place to live and was promised a job as a rocker in the building business.

Joy! Thanksgiving! Praise! And rightly so. Soon Rich and Becky made the exciting move. Shortly after their arrival, however, construction ground to a halt. No work. No income. Rent due. To add to the situation, the baby was due in a few months. Now did they still believe God directed the move? Had it really been His will?

Subsequent events have proved the answer to be a resounding yes. But it was not all that clear when things fell apart around them. Although all they had were a few promises that God had given them from His Word, they held on by faith and God saw them through their difficulties.

Problems of this sort happen to the best of Christians; they happened to the Apostle Paul. "During the night Paul had a vision of a man of Macedonia standing and begging him, 'Come over to Macedonia and help us.' After Paul had seen the vision, we got ready at once to leave for Macedonia, concluding that God had called us to preach the Gospel to them" (Acts 16:9-10). Here was a divine call to do God's work among people chosen by Him to hear the Gospel. What could they expect when they arrived? Would a brass band welcome them? Would thousands of people eager to repent throng the shores?

What actually happened was quite different. The only immediate results Paul saw were the conversion of Lydia, the spiritual release of an unfortunate girl caught up in the occult, and a jail sentence accompanied by a whipping that left him and Silas sitting in the stocks in pain.

What was Paul's response when the going got rough? Did he doubt whether God had really brought them there? "About midnight Paul and Silas were praying and singing hymns to God, and the other prisoners were listening to them" (Acts 16:25). He was still full of faith, as evidenced by his songs of praise and thanksgiving. God was all he and Silas needed.

TRUSTING WHEN THINGS GO WRONG

When the Israelites grumbled against Moses and Aaron in the wilderness, their murmurings were really against God (Exodus 16:8). Likewise, our practical belief in the sovereignty of God is really tested when someone does something we don't like or something happens to make our lives difficult. Perhaps our spiritual leader asks us to do something we'd rather not do, or does something himself that we think is wrong. Even if we don't murmur aloud as the Hebrews did, we have silent conversations in our hearts, mentally criticizing or complaining. Mental argument is one of the easiest things in the world to fall into, because we can always put down the other person.

I personally learned a lesson about the dangers of a complaining spirit in the early 1950's which has stuck with me through the years. During the first two years of my Christian life, my wife, Virginia, and I attended Northwestern College in Minneapolis. There we met Don Rosenberger, the local Navigator representative. He was teaching courses in Bible study and follow-up in the college, and Virginia and I were in his classes. He soon took a special interest in us and helped us in our walk with the Lord. A remarkably gifted teacher and leader, Don usually had a half dozen things going at once, and it was a challenge to be involved with him.

At the beginning of my third year at Northwestern, Dawson Trotman asked me to move to Seattle, become involved in the Navigator ministry, and live with Gordy and Chris Donaldson. Gordy was a godly man and a producer of disciples. He walked circumspectly and quietly through life. He was just the opposite of Don in temperament. Whenever he would do something, I would criticize him in my mind: *That's not the way Rosenberger would do it.* Of course there was a simple and obvious reason for his not doing it as Don did. There was only one Don Rosenberger. Nobody else was supposed to be like Don, but in my immaturity I didn't understand that.

The following summer I attended a conference where Don was speaking. As soon as I got some time with him, I began complaining about Gordon. He listened patiently,

heard me out, and then said, "Let me show you a verse."
He opened his Bible and read to me, "Then Miriam and
Aaron spoke against Moses . . . And the Lord heard it"
(Numbers 12:1-2).

Looking me straight in the eye, he said, "God has
heard all your murmuring and complaining. He has heard
what you said today. He has heard all the conversation
you have had with yourself in mental argument." Then for
about an hour he explained to me why the Lord couldn't
use a guy like me. I had hoped to work with The Navigators when I had finished my training, but now my
dreams were shattered. The Navigators didn't need mur-
murers and complainers. Crushed in spirit, I went out on
the side of a mountain and spent a long time in prayer.

After I returned to the conference center, I began
talking to a friend named Bob Glockner who was also
having some spiritual struggles. We decided to get together to pray and went to the ball field to be alone with
the Lord. The dust was about four inches thick, and Bob
suggested we lie face down in the dust to show our true
humility and repentant spirit. So we did. I can still see Bob
lying on the ground, his face buried in the dust. I glanced
over as he was praying and could see little puffs of dust
rising with his prayers.

Suddenly the chapel bell rang, signaling that we had 10
minutes to get to the meeting. Since nobody was ever late
for meetings in those days, we jumped up, dusted ourselves off, and ran for the chapel. Just as we rounded the
corner of the building, Dawson Trotman reached out and
grabbed me by the arm. "Let me ask you a question," he
said. "How would you like to be in D.C. with Rosenberger next year?" Praise God! I was pardoned! God had
forgiven my sin and taught me something about His
sovereignty. He was giving me another chance.

Doctrinally, I can say that I believe in the sovereignty of God, that He controls and directs all of His creation. It is an easy doctrine to believe in and to explain. The real question, however, is, "Do I believe in the sovereignty of God in my current situation? Is God guiding me now?" That's where the crunch comes.

The Scriptures abound with statements that affirm His sovereignty. Mrs. Lila Trotman has shared a verse with people all over the world, especially when troubles and testings arise. It provides a short, simple statement of God's authority in His universe. "But our God is in the heavens; He does whatever He pleases" (Psalm 115:3). He plans and acts after the counsel of His own will. Simply stated, God is in charge of everything all the time.

Betty Skinner, in her excellent book *Daws,* the story of Dawson Trotman and The Navigators, describes how the organization was led of God to make its home at Glen Eyrie in Colorado Springs. She tells how Daws came to the Glen, climbed to the top of Razorback Ridge, a chain of rocks overlooking the estate, and made a covenant with God. "Lord, if You will entrust all this to us, I want to dedicate it now to You as David did, to be used for Your glory, to make known Your holy name in all the world." With his Bible open, he scratched a reference on the sandstone rock face to witness his pledge.

The passage that Daws carved on that rock includes the following reference to the sovereignty of God: "Thine is the dominion, O Lord, and Thou dost exalt Thyself as head over all. Both riches and honor come from Thee, and Thou dost rule over all, and in Thy hand is power and might; and it lies in Thy hand to make great, and to strengthen everyone. Now therefore, our God, we thank Thee, and praise Thy glorious name" (1 Chronicles 29:11-13).

The Israelites actually accused Moses of bringing them into the wilderness to kill them. When people are upset and nervous, their minds don't function properly. Moses had killed an Egyptian *for* them; he wasn't going to try to kill *them*. He had done everything he knew to do and yet was angrily told, "You brought us out here to kill us." If you become a leader in your Sunday School or church, you will find that if you do 17 things right and one thing wrong, people will remember that one wrong thing. Moses, too, had done many things for the Israelites and yet they criticized him.

Had God wanted to kill these people, He wouldn't have had to take them into the wilderness. He could have easily disposed of them at the Red Sea. There, surrounded by eight billion tons of water (give or take a few tons), only His hand lay between them and certain death. All He had to do was release the sea, and it would have been all over.

In answer to the people's complaint of imminent starvation, God said, "Behold, I will rain bread from heaven for you; and the people shall go out and gather a day's portion every day, that I may test them, whether or not they will walk in My instruction" (Exodus 16:4).

God was going to supply their food in a way that would continually test their faith and obedience. They were commanded to gather enough manna for only one day at a time. They were to obey God, trusting Him for each new day's supply.

The coin of our Christian lives has these same two sides: faith and obedience. Our walk with God boils down to two things: a childlike reliance on God—His goodness, His watchcare, His promises, His grace and mercy—and a God-given desire to serve Him and our generation according to His will. We must never be deluded into thinking we can trust God, and then live as we choose with self at the center of things. That is not trusting God; it is mocking Him. Nor must we try to do good in our own strength and wisdom with little or no reliance on Him. Simply stated, we must trust *and* obey.

The fluctuations of life affect everyone. During a severe trial, you will not likely doubt that God exists. But you may doubt His goodness. You may say to yourself, *If God really loves me, why has this come about?* The love of God will then become a cold, sterile doctrine with no reality in your life.

The mistake you made was to ask the question "Why?" Quite possibly you will never know all the reasons for what transpires. That's OK. God does. And He may or may not choose to let you in on it. That's up to Him. He knows best and He loves you.

Sometimes life is like looking at the underside of a woven rug. All you see is a jumble of knots and strings. The pattern can be seen only from the top. Likewise, someday you will understand when God takes you to Himself, makes it all plain, and says, "Well done!" The one question God never answered for Job was the question "Why?" Job had to go through his ordeal without understanding what was behind it all. So if that happens to you, cheer up. You're in good company.

The power of God—as well as His goodness—can also come into question. As the situation grows more and more hopeless, you grow more and more helpless. You tell yourself the problem can't get any worse, but it does and you are overcome with remorse and shame. Finally you reach the point where you're convinced that even God can't do anything about it. Your life is so snarled with heartache, hopelessness, and fear that you feel like a rat in a maze. You face a blank wall at every turn. The devil accuses and mocks you. You cry out for relief and no relief comes. Yet, though you may think God has forgotten you, He hasn't. He is trying to build genuine faith into your life that will stand the severest tests.

Jesus constantly taught this principle to His disciples. One day, for example, Jesus said to His disciples, "Let's go over to the other side of the lake." So they got into a boat. As they sailed, Jesus fell asleep. A squall came down on the lake and the boat began to take in water. Terrified, the disciples woke Him, crying, "Master, Master, we're going to drown!" Getting up, He rebuked the wind and the raging waters; the storm subsided, and all was calm. "Where is your faith?" He then asked the amazed disciples (Luke 8:22-25).

Note that Jesus first rebuked the wind and the waves and then rebuked His disciples for their lack of faith. Why? If they had remembered and trusted what He had said, they would not have worried. Did He say, "Let's go out into the middle of the lake and drown"? No. He simply said, "Let's go over to the other side." When Jesus sets out to take you to the other side, He will do it, regardless of wind and waves.

TRUST AND KEEP ON TRUSTING

Moses' reply to the Israelites when they grumbled about starving demonstrates his great leadership. He did not say, "Well, of course I don't know for sure, but God *says* He's going to give you flesh and bread." Stepping out in faith, he said in effect, "There will be bread; you can count on it" (see Exodus 16:8). Although he couldn't see any flesh or bread, he knew they would be given because God had promised them.

Daniel demonstrated the same kind of faith when he

told King Nebuchadnezzar that, given a little time, he would show the king the interpretation of his dream (Daniel 2:16). Daniel didn't say, "I might be able to do it." He said he would do it. That's faith. God requires such steps of all of us.

After God had provided quail and manna (Exodus 16:4-36), a new problem arose. "Then all the congregation of the sons of Israel journeyed by stages from the wilderness of Sin, according to the command of the Lord, and camped at Rephidim, and there was no water for the people to drink. Therefore the people quarreled with Moses and said, 'Give us water that we may drink.' And Moses said to them, 'Why do you quarrel with me? Why do you test the Lord?' " (Exodus 17:1-2)

First there was no food; now there was no water. So the people sent for Moses and demanded water. Why? Was he standing beside a water cooler? Did Moses control a caravan of camels loaded down with water barrels? Did he have a giant well-digging rig in his possession? No. He was in the same predicament they were—surrounded by hot, dry, burning sand that stretched as far as the eye could see. They came to Moses because they were desperate people, facing death in the wilderness. They came to him because they had nowhere else to turn.

One summer our family was visiting my mother's home. During early evening the clouds began to swirl, the wind began to blow, and the rains came. Suddenly a lightning bolt struck the telephone pole in the alley behind our house, accompanied by the loudest thunderclap I have ever heard. My wife and three children leaped in my direction. My youngest jumped straight up into my arms. Why? I was as rattled as they were. Simple. They had nowhere else to turn, and I was a point of security and safety for them. Even though I couldn't really *do* anything for them, they still turned to me. The same was true with the Israelites when they found themselves in a desperate situation. Moses was the only one who might know what to do.

"But the people thirsted there for water; and they grumbled against Moses and said, 'Why, now, have you brought us up from Egypt, to kill us and our children and our livestock with thirst?' So Moses cried out to the Lord, saying, 'What shall I do to this people? A little more and they will stone me' " (Exodus 17:3-4).

What was God's response? In effect He said, "I know that they're about ready to stone you; I understand that you think it's almost over for you. But here's what you are to do: take your staff and beat it on the rock."

Farfetched? But he did it, and the water came out of the rock. If you read the cross-references on this point, you'll see some amazing things. "He split the rocks in the wilderness, and gave them abundant drink like the ocean depths. He brought forth streams also from the rock, and caused waters to run down like rivers" (Psalm 78:15-16). This wasn't a mere trickle; a tremendous, raging river came gushing out of that rock. It had to be quite a flow to provide water for such a huge caravan of people and animals.

Jesus Himself met these people at their point of need. He gave them the water—symbolizing His own life-giving spiritual presence with them—and satisfied their thirst. He calmed their fears and gave them hope. Only Jesus could do that for them and only He can do that for us. "They drank from the spiritual rock that accompanied them, and that rock was Christ" (1 Corinthians 10:4). He is the only source of spiritual life, nourishment, and truth in this world. Many learned philosophers and their philosophies come and go. Theories about life and the afterlife appear and disappear. Scientific ideas are promoted and then rejected. But Jesus remains "the same yesterday and today and forever" (Hebrews 13:8).

Jesus' own teaching clearly illustrates this dramatic truth. "On the last and greatest day of the Feast, Jesus stood and said in a loud voice, 'If a man is thirsty, let him come to Me and drink' " (John 7:37). Some months earlier He had spoken to the woman at the well, "Everyone who drinks this water will be thirsty again, but whoever drinks the water I give him will never thirst. Indeed, the water I give him will become in him a spring of water welling up to everlasting life" (John 4:13-14). Century follows century and the resources of Christ never fail.

As you and I live our lives before the Lord, He will occasionally test our faith, even as He tested the children of Israel in the wilderness. If we say we love Him, He will give us opportunities to demonstrate the truth of our words. If we say we trust Him, He will provide the tests whereby our faith can be proved genuine and then deepened. But we have the assurance that the tests will never overwhelm us. "No temptation has seized you except what is common to man. And God is faithful; He will not let you be tempted beyond what you can bear. But when you are tempted, He will also provide a way out so that you can stand up under it" (1 Corinthians 10:13).

God knows our limits and our capacities for growth. So if He has brought a severe test your way, rest in the confidence of His promises. "Do not fear, for I am with you; do not anxiously look about you, for I am your God. I will strengthen you, surely I will help you, surely I will uphold you with My righteous right hand" (Isaiah 41:10).

If your life needs a special touch of His refreshing presence, trust Him for it. "The afflicted and needy are seeking water, but there is none, and their tongue is parched with thirst; I the Lord will answer them Myself, as the God of Israel I will not forsake them. I will open rivers on the bare heights, and springs in the midst of the valleys; I will make the wilderness a pool of water, and the dry land fountains of water" (Isaiah 41:17-18).

Do you need strength for today? "He gives strength to the weary, and to him who lacks might He increases power. Though youths grow weary and tired, and vigorous young men stumble badly, yet those who wait for the Lord will gain new strength; they will mount up with wings like eagles, they will run and not get tired, they will walk and not become weary" (Isaiah 40:29-31).

If you're not sure which is the right path for you to take, the indispensable ingredient on your part is faith. "Trust in the Lord with all your heart, and do not lean on your own understanding. In all your ways acknowledge Him, and He will make your paths straight" (Proverbs 3:5-6).

The same principle applied to the Israelites during their sojourn in the wilderness. Vital and important lessons were to follow, but the primary lesson they needed to learn was to apply their faith in God to their daily lives.

TOPICS FOR STUDY

1. Abraham, the man of faith (Genesis 12—22).
2. The heroes of the faith (Hebrews 11).
3. The development of faith in the disciples of Jesus (the Gospels).
4. Isaiah's call to faith in a faithful God (Isaiah 40—66).
5. Faith in the Early Church (the Book of Acts).
6. The place of faith in the Gospel (the Book of Romans).

APPLICATION: What truths do I need to apply to my life from this chapter? How will I go about it?

CHAPTER THREE

RESPONSIBILITIES
The Lesson in Duty

Study Material: Exodus 18—24

M ANY years after it happened, the Apostle Peter still vividly remembered one of his most outstanding experiences—witnessing the transfiguration of Jesus Christ. "When we were with Him on the holy mount," he wrote, "we saw this and we saw that and I experienced something wonderful. But let me tell you something: we have in our hands right now a more sure word of prophecy that you should pay careful attention to" (2 Peter 1:18-19, paraphrased). The "more sure word" to which Peter referred was the Old Testament, which had been written by holy men of God moved by the Holy Spirit (1:20-21).

As we accordingly study selected Old Testament passages, we will learn many valuable lessons. In the preceding chapter, we observed how God taught His people a valuable and life-lasting lesson on faith. The second lesson He taught them was the responsibility of duty.

THE DUTY OF LEADERSHIP

Before God could teach His people the responsibility of duty, He first needed to prepare Moses to be a dynamic, responsible leader. This would have an important bearing on what happened later, for lessons first have to be learned by those who lead. "It came about the next day that Moses sat to judge the people, and the people stood about Moses from the morning until the evening" (Exodus 18:13). Moses was hard at work being the leader he was meant to be. Or so he thought.

Moses was in constant, vital contact with the people. Even though they had misused and opposed him, Moses was involved directly with the people. In spite of their earlier attempt to stone him (see Exodus 17:4), he was out there day after day, giving his life to them and sharing himself with them. Once, when I had read this passage, I jotted in the margin of my Bible, "Though others fail us, we must not fail them." He was not the kind of a leader who holds himself aloof and delegates responsibility to others. And that is a great strength in leadership, for people will generally follow a leader whom they know firsthand.

Jethro, Moses' father-in-law, watched him go through an impossibly long schedule day after day. Finally, unable to take it any longer, he asked, "What is this thing that you are doing for the people? Why do you alone sit as judge and all the people stand about you from morning until evening?" (Exodus 18:14)

Moses had his answer ready. "When they have a dispute, it comes to me, and I judge between a man and his neighbor, and make known the statutes of God and His laws" (18:16). What was Moses basically saying to his father-in-law by these words—and to everyone by his actions? "I'm indispensable, for I'm the one with the answers from God."

Then came Jethro's wise and classic reply. "The thing that you are doing is not good. You will surely wear out, both yourself and these people who are with you, for the task is too heavy for you; you cannot do it alone. Now listen to me: I shall give you counsel" (18:17-19). Moses was not only harming himself being a workaholic; he would eventually harm the people as well.

"You are going to counsel me?" Moses could have answered his father-in-law piously. "I get my counsel directly from God." That would have been a natural, normal response. Moses, however, was a wise man, and a wise man seeks to increase his learning. If a person consistently refuses good counsel, he is in deep trouble.

Since Moses was open to counsel, Jethro continued, "You be the people's representative before God, and you bring the disputes to God, then teach them the statutes and the laws, and make known to them the way in which they are to walk, and the work they are to do" (18:19-20). Jethro taught Moses a lesson concerning one of the duties of leadership—communication.

Jethro then shared with Moses the principle of delegation. "Furthermore, you shall select out of all the people able men who fear God, men of truth, those who hate dishonest gain; and you shall place these over them, as leaders of thousands, of hundreds, of fifties and of tens. And let them judge the people at all times; and let it be that every major dispute they will bring to you, but every minor dispute they themselves will judge. So it will be easier for you, and they will bear the burden with you" (18:21-22).

These passages have been a great help to me in the leadership responsibilities God has committed to me. Moses' first and foremost responsibility as a leader was to pray for the people. Second, he was to be a teacher, instructing the people in the statutes and laws of God. Third, he was to show them the way in which they were to walk and the work they were to do. Fourth, he had to delegate some of his individual responsibilities to others.

Lessons like these are not so much taught as caught. Kenny Watters, who now serves with Wycliffe Bible Translators, led Don Rosenberger to Christ while they were both in the Navy, stationed at Pearl Harbor shortly after the attack by the Japanese.

Before long Don noticed that Kenny came to work a half hour early each day to read the Bible that he kept in his desk drawer. So Don bought a Bible, put it in his desk drawer, and began to come to work a half hour early each day to read it.

Kenny had another strange practice which aroused Don's curiosity. After work, Kenny would head for a grassy slope overlooking the harbor. One afternoon Don followed Kenny and saw him lie down on his back in a secluded spot halfway up the hill. Don remained hidden, but crept close enough to hear Kenny praying. After listening long enough to get the hang of it, Don silently crept away to another spot on the hillside and began what was to develop into a powerful and productive prayer life.

Moses, according to Jethro, was to teach the people certain things. He was to "make known the way in which they are to walk," referring to their personal lives, and "the work they are to do," referring to their ministries (see 18:20). In that day as well as in our own, people learned more by looking to a good example than by listening to words alone.

All of us as leaders need to be pacesetters, people who are living examples of the truth of God we are trying to convey. Consequently the person who is being taught can see God's truth in action. The Apostle Paul said, "Follow my example, as I follow the example of Christ" (1 Corinthians 11:1).

"So Moses listened to his father-in-law, and did all that he had said" (Exodus 18:24). Now that Moses had learned what his responsibilities were to the people, he could, in turn, teach them their duties—to God and to other people.

DUTIES OF THE PEOPLE

Think with me for a moment. When was the last time you heard a message or read an article or book on the Ten Commandments? We don't often hear of man's duty to God and to his fellowman, principles epitomized in the Commandments. Is this shortage of messages and material an overreaction to the older forms of legalism that were so sterile and stifling? Possibly. But has the liberty and freedom of the New Testament replaced legalism? No, too often the pendulum has swung all the way and has replaced legalism with *license*. If in reaction against oppressive legalism we have become lawless, we certainly haven't gained any ground.

There is a flaw in our thinking when we perceive the Law of God negatively. The Ten Commandments were given for our welfare and our good, not for our detriment and our hurt. Certain restrictions are a necessary part of life. Traffic laws save thousands from unnecessary death on the streets and highways. Drug laws protect people from taking an overdose or from taking the wrong medicine.

Furthermore, God has not repealed these commands. Skip Gray, who carries a major responsibility for The Navigators on the East Coast of the United States, points out that the Lord has repeated every one of them in the New Testament. Check these references:

- Commandments One and Two—Matthew 4:10
- Commandment Three—James 5:12 and Matthew 5:33-37
- Commandment Four—Acts 20:7 (many other references show the Early Church setting aside one day in seven for worship of God and rest from its labors)
- Commandment Five—Ephesians 6:1-3
- Commandment Six—Matthew 5:21-22; 1 John 3:15
- Commandment Seven—Galatians 5:19-21; Ephesians 5:3; Hebrews 13:4
- Commandment Eight—Ephesians 4:28
- Commandment Nine—Matthew 15:19; Ephesians 4:25
- Commandment Ten—Luke 12:15; 1 Timothy 6:10; Romans 7:7

It is obvious from these and many other New Testament passages that God still thinks highly of His standards. He has not repealed the Law He gave to govern every soul in this world; He demands our obedience. But He has also put His love in our hearts by His Spirit to enable us to keep the Law.

In His Law God emphasized love for one another. "Let no debt remain outstanding, except the continuing debt to love one another, for he who loves his fellow man has fulfilled the law. The commandments, 'Do not commit adultery,' 'Do not murder,' 'Do not steal,' 'Do not covet,' and whatever other commandment there may be, are summed up in this one rule: 'Love your neighbor as yourself.' Love does no harm to its neighbor. Therefore love is the fulfillment of the law" (Romans 13:8-10).

Obviously, if I love my neighbor I will not kill him, lie about him, steal from him, and so on. And even more obviously, if I love God, I will honor, reverence, and worship Him. Jesus Christ came and took up residence in our hearts to lead us toward God's commands, to enable us to keep them.

DUTIES TO GOD

After the people had been prepared to receive God's Law (Exodus 19), the word came to them. "I am the Lord your God, who brought you out of the land of Egypt, out of the house of slavery" (20:2). God wanted them to remember who was giving them these laws. He was their Deliverer. He brought them out of their bondage in Egypt. Everything God was about to tell His people was based on His mercy and grace. In effect He was saying,"Do you remember those taskmasters with their whips? I delivered you from them! Do you remember the weary hours, the unbearable fatigue, the hopelessness and despair? I delivered you! I am the One who brought you out of all that. I have demonstrated My grace, My mercy, and My love. And now, for us to fellowship together, here is what I expect of you."

The duty we're talking about, the duty of keeping the Ten Commandments, is a response of love to the One who has done something wonderful for His people.

God's mercy keeps us from the judgment we rightfully deserve; His grace showers blessings on us that we don't deserve. That's quite a combination. Put mercy and grace together, basing the whole thing on love, and you have a great deal going for you. Israel had that combination, and so does every Christian. Based on that relationship, what does God expect from us?

Commandments One and Two

"You shall have no other gods before Me. You shall not make for yourself an idol, or any likeness of what is in heaven above or on the earth beneath or in the water under the earth. You shall not worship them or serve them" (Exodus 20:3-5). God forbids anything to come between Him and us, and He forbids us to make any images of Him or anything else to worship. Why? Why did God begin by forbidding idolatry? Because there are no more gods; there is only one.

The practical problem, however, is in loving anything more than you love God. And that is possible. There are things you can put in God's place, but He says not to do it. God does not want first place in our worship; He wants the only place. If there is God, then there is no second place. There is God—period. When people speak of God having first place in their lives, you sometimes get the idea that something else is running a close second.

Imagine my going to Dallas, calling home, and saying, "Sweetheart, I'm having a great time down here; everything is going well. By the way, I went out with another woman and had a good time, but don't worry, you're still first." Then I go to New Orleans, and call home and say the same thing. Then the same from New York City. No way. Virginia doesn't want to be the first woman in my life; she wants to be the only woman. And she is.

What can compete with God? Money? Fame? Power? Pleasure? There is absolutely nothing you can place in the same category as God, and there is nothing that can compete with Him. He must have the only place in our lives.

Then God talks about serving idols. "You shall not worship them or serve them" (Exodus 20:5). Obviously we can do that which is right in the sight of God and still do it with an imperfect heart (see 1 Corinthians 13:1-3). However, there is no moral value in anything we do which is based on a wrong motive.

One way to walk in victory is to do what is right and to be sorry when we don't. But we must do what is right out of a sense of love for God, not out of a sense of duty.

In a well-known comic strip, Dennis the Menace went out into the yard where his mother was working and asked, "It's Valentine Day, isn't it Mom?" Getting an affirmative reply, he went into the house to make her a Valentine while she continued to work in the yard.

Suddenly she realized what was going on and rushed into the house; but she was too late. The mess was appalling—paper, ink, glue, scraps all over the place. Innocent Dennis then handed her his messy, homemade card and said proudly, "Here, Mom, this is for you because I love you."

In the next frame, Dennis asked, "Hey, Mom, why are you squeezing me so hard?" And in the final frame, his mother answered, "Because I love you too, Dennis." Did Dennis do the right thing? No, but his mother accepted his action, and its unfortunate byproducts, because it was prompted by love.

We are all like Dennis. We've got it in our hearts to serve God. Imperfectly, perhaps, but we do it because we love Him, because He saved us from our sins. He is the Lord our God, who has delivered us out of slavery. And when we respond in love with an act of service for Him, God accepts it—imperfect though it may be.

Now this is not to advocate slovenly service for the Lord. We must be careful to do our best in any given situation. But God's primary interest is in our hearts, our love, our devotion. These will lead us to desire to serve Him—to do what He wants us to do—whenever He wants us to do it.

Commandment Three

"You shall not take the name of the Lord your God in vain, for the Lord will not leave him unpunished who takes His name in vain" (Exodus 20:7). Nobody can speak lightly of God without also thinking lightly of God. He is holy, omniscient, omnipresent, omnipotent, and much more. Even though He has entered into a living, vital, warm, loving, heart-to-heart relationship with us, the fact remains that He is not the "Man upstairs." We don't have a merely casual relationship with God. He is holy and righteous. Proper reverence for God will never permit us to take His name in vain.

Commandment Four

"Remember the sabbath day, to keep it holy. Six days you shall labor and do all your work, but the seventh day is a sabbath of the Lord your God; in it you shall not do any work" (Exodus 20:8-10). Here God is helping us regulate our lives in such a way that we can produce the most. He tells us that if we will set aside a certain portion of our time for Him, we'll get much more done in the rest of our time.

Dawson Trotman worked with a man once who was part of a witnessing team. The man's desire waned and before long he dropped out altogether. Daws discovered that the man had begun to use the Lord's day for his own pleasure and not for the Lord. This, of course, is something we must be careful to note in the lives of people with whom we are working. When the desire level falls below the level of commitment required to carry on the ministry, trouble is brewing. Either the person will carry on in the energy of the flesh, or he will drop out.

After this man dropped out, Daws looked him up and gave him this verse: "If because of the sabbath, you turn your foot from doing your own pleasure on My holy day, and call the sabbath a delight, the holy of the Lord honorable, and shall honor it, desisting from your own ways, from seeking your own pleasure, and speaking your own word, then you will take delight in the Lord, and I will make you ride on the heights of the earth; and I will feed you with the heritage of Jacob your father, for the mouth of the Lord has spoken" (Isaiah 58:13-14). As a result, this man became motivated to serve God and was restored to fellowship with the Lord and to a life of fruitful service for Him.

Throughout Scripture, God encourages us to set aside one day in seven just for Him. If we do, we'll accomplish much more during the rest of our time. Those of us who have been willing to try it know the truth of that statement by experience.

DUTIES TO ONE ANOTHER

The next six commandments deal with the responsibilities we should have toward one another. If we are to love God totally, then we must love others in His family as well.

Commandment Five

"Honor your father and your mother, that your days may be prolonged in the land which the Lord your God gives you" (Exodus 20:12). This command to honor is basic to the home relationship. We honor another family member in many ways, but the key is to take that person into our lives. It is up to the parents to set the pace, to show their children how to show honor.

Once when I was flying to Chicago, I wrote a letter to Randy, my younger son, who was in Hawaii as part of a Navigator summer training program. I told him about our cat, which had been unusually obedient lately, and described the roses and the corn in the garden. None of my news was earth-shakingly important. What I was doing, however, was taking Randy into my life. I was following the advice of Pliny the Younger (A.D. 62-113), who once wrote a friend, "You say there is nothing to write about. Then write to me that there is nothing to write about."

Very few people do such things because they seem so simple, so incidental, and so foolish. But they are not. Such applications of honor teach children to take their parents into *their* lives.

Applications of honor also affect marital relationships. The Apostle Paul wrote, "However, each one of you [husbands] also must love his wife as he loves himself, and the wife must respect her husband" (Ephesians 5:33). Peter also dealt with the husband-wife relationship. "Husbands . . . try to understand the wives you live with, honoring them as physically weaker yet equally heirs with you of the grace of life" (1 Peter 3:7, PH). A poll taken among a group of wives asked what they wished their husbands would do that they were not already doing. The nearly unanimous answer was that they wanted their husbands to show them small courtesies, such as holding the chair at the table and opening the car door.

Actually, the "honor principle" applies to the whole broad sweep of family relationships. Husbands should honor their wives, wives should honor their husbands, parents should honor their children, and this will teach the children to honor their parents.

You've got quite a thing going if you work on that. The wife is thinking of little ways she can show honor to her husband. The husband is thinking of little ways he can show honor to his wife. The parents are sharing the Lord and their lives with their kids. The children are thinking of ways they can honor their parents. Put all that together, and you've got a household in which mutual honor prevails.

The little things really count. What sticks in your memory? If you are like most people, you remember the time a friend made a special effort to come by and see you when you were sick. Or the time your family returned from a trip and your neighbor brought a casserole over for supper. Or the time you were going to be in a wedding and your son offered to shine your shoes.

I know a family that has one rule regarding the exchange of gifts at Christmastime: the gift must not cost anything. They draw names and then think of something nice they can do for that person during the coming year. Nothing big. Just some little thing that will help the person in some way and make life a little brighter.

As the old hymn says:

Do not wait until some deed of greatness you may do,
Do not wait to shed your light afar;
To the many duties ever near you now be true,
Brighten the corner where you are.

Few of us will ever do great deeds and be remembered by history. But all of us can do some little thing that will cheer a heart and brighten a day. And bring honor.

Commandment Six

"You shall not murder" (Exodus 20:13). To God, life is sacred. When a life is snuffed out, something has just stopped that goes all the way back to Adam.

The teaching of Jesus Christ takes us to the heart of this commandment. He said, "You have heard that it was said to the people long ago, 'Do not murder, and anyone who murders will be subject to judgment.' But I tell you

that anyone who is angry with his brother will be subject
to judgment" (Matthew 5:21-22). When Cain killed his
brother, it was not a sudden thing; it had begun with anger
in his heart.

We can destroy a person in many ways without killing
him. To call a man a fool is to rob him of his good name,
which is better than life. We all know of people who
endure a living hell because someone they love ignores
them, looks down on them, or makes fun of them in front
of others. Life is sacred. God forbids destroying a life in
any way, whether by an unkind remark, harmful act, or an
overbearing or hateful spirit.

Commandment Seven

"You shall not commit adultery" (Exodus 20:14). Purity
of life is important, but how are we to keep pure? "So I
say, live by the Spirit, and you will not gratify the desires
of your sinful nature" (Galatians 5:16). The "desires of
your sinful nature" here are the lusts of the flesh, which
include sexual impurity.

I used to be terrified of flying. My work occasionally
required that I travel by airplane, and I hated it. Frankly, I
would rather have taken a beating. During one such flight,
I was sitting next to a pilot, and he began to explain to me
what was happening. As we rolled down the runway, he
explained that because of the shape of the wing there was
a "lift" developing. "When the plane gains a certain
speed," he said, "the power of the lift is greater than the
force of gravity, and the plane becomes airborne." He
seemed so confident and matter-of-fact about it, and it all
sounded so reasonable, that I began to relax.

As I've thought about the principle of "lift," I have
seen how it applies to our lives. As we move ahead in

the Spirit, we overcome the downward drag of the flesh. You can test that out. Start "moving ahead" in the things of God and see if they don't provide enough "lift" to keep you from the pull of the world, the flesh, and the devil.

Few people have a problem with the lust of the flesh while on their knees praying over a sick child. Why? Because prayer is a matter of the Spirit, and keeps you from dwelling on the things of the flesh.

Being busy is not necessarily the key to spiritual victory. Fellowship with and obedience to Christ results in spiritual victory. This means that we must be active and involved in such things of the Spirit as Bible study, prayer, witnessing, and so on. These activities will be used by Him to help us obey the Seventh Commandment.

Commandment Eight

"You shall not steal" (Exodus 20:15). Honesty is not always easy. You are traveling and spend some money. Is it a business expense or not? You can put it on one side of the ledger or on the other.

Little tests of our honesty come from many sources. I remember a one-day conference I had in Denver. It was a hot day, everyone else was in a workshop, and a friend and I were thirsty. So we walked down to a gas station to buy soft drinks. Bob put in his dime (it was 10¢ in those days), the machine went "kalunk," he pulled a lever, and out came the bottle. I put in a nickel and was ready to put in the other one when the machine went "kalunk" and spewed out my bottle of pop.

Pretty good, I thought. *One nickel and a bottle of pop.* But then God said quietly, "LeRoy, that is *not* your nickel." I have never wanted a nickel so badly in my whole life as I wanted that nickel. I coveted it. But I went to the station attendant, told him about the machine, and gave him the nickel.

He responded, "An honest man!"

This principle applies to other areas of life as well. It is easy, for example, to take credit for what someone else has done, to understate or overstate the case, and steal another's reputation. There is so much more to stealing than robbing a bank. We must be on guard all the time.

Commandment Nine

"You shall not bear false witness against your neighbor" (Exodus 20:16). This, of course, can take many forms. Lying. Gossip. A whispering campaign. False accusation. Overstatements. I have seen a man driven from an organization because of half truths and subtle suggestions of wrongdoing. A false witness can be devastating.

This commandment also deals with just plain lying— with intent to deceive. It is easy to boast of works we haven't done, to promise something and not do it and then make excuses, or to make a report of something sound better than it really is.

My mother used to say, "Tell the truth and shame the devil." As a boy I never understood that, but I think I'm finally beginning to see the picture. If we are to get along well in the everyday affairs of life and walk with the Lord, we must be truthful. When we lie, the devil, who is the father of lies, injures our usefulness as citizens and Christians. When we tell the truth, we shame the devil.

Commandment Ten

"You shall not covet your neighbor's house; you shall not covet your neighbor's wife or his male servant or his female servant or his ox or his donkey or anything that belongs to your neighbor" (Exodus 20:17). Essentially, covetousness accuses God of mismanagement. Since God owns everything, He decides what to allot to you and what to others. When we covet, we are arguing with God about the way He is managing His affairs.

The antidote to covetousness is giving. "Give, and it will be given to you. A good measure, pressed down, shaken together and running over, will be poured into your lap. For with the measure you use, it will be measured to you" (Luke 6:38). As Christians, we are essentially God's delivery system; we are His United Parcel Service. When it comes to material things, we deliver for God to the needy around us. Since material things often corrupt us, God is limited as to how much He can pass through our hands because of our tendency to stop the flow and siphon off the abundance for ourselves. Once we have that problem licked, however, it's amazing how much God can flow through our lives. We ought to be eager for God to maximize His plan for world evangelization through us.

Heaven is just bursting with blessings for those who are generous, those who do not covet. It is like a granary that's jammed full, just waiting to be opened and spill out the grain. God is eager to open the windows of heaven and spread the blessings around. Aladdin had only to rub the magic lamp and the genie appeared; Ali Baba just said, "Open Sesame!" All the Christian has to do with God is learn to give, to be generous. " 'Bring the whole tithe into the storehouse, so that there may be food in My house, and test Me now in this,' says the Lord of hosts, 'if I will not open for you the windows of heaven, and pour out for you a blessing until there is no more need' " (Malachi 3:10).

SUMMARY

The commandments of God are an expression of His nature. Yet since the Garden of Eden, men have chafed against divine limitations.

God left clearly stated, concise, and understandable instructions to keep us on track. When we hear or read them, we instinctively know they are right and good. They have a ring of truth about them. They encompass the essence of our responsibilities to God and to our fellowmen. The people of Israel understood this, and on three occasions replied, "We will do them and be obedient" (see Exodus 19:8; 24:3, 7).

To the Christian, God gives grace and empowerment to obey these commandments and to hold them in deep respect. He also says, "Keep My commandments and live, and My teaching as the apple of your eye. Bind them on your fingers; write them on the tablet of your heart" (Proverbs 7:2-3). The lesson in duty that the people of Israel learned in the wilderness—duty based on the wonderful redemption God had provided for them—is the same lesson we can learn today.

TOPICS FOR STUDY

1. Leadership responsibilities (Acts 20; 1 Timothy 3; Titus 1).
2. The New Testament's repetition of the Ten Commandments.
3. Duties to God (see Matthew 22:36-40).
4. Duties to fellowmen (see Matthew 22:36-40).
5. The concept of Law in the Book of Galatians.
6. The concept of Covenant and its responsibilities in both the Old and New Testaments.

APPLICATION: What aspects of my duty to God and my duties to my fellowmen do I need to apply from the lessons of this chapter? How am I going to do it?

CHAPTER FOUR

YOU NEVER STAND TALLER
The Lesson in Worship

*Study Material: Exodus 25—40; Psalm 119; Mark 10:17-22
Luke 9:23; Romans 12:1-2; 2 Timothy 3:16-17*

STEP by step, God led Israel through His training program in the wilderness. The battles ahead would tax
His people to their limits; their training had to be precise
and complete. Slowly but surely, He was preparing them
to meet the enemy and emerge victorious.

One grand and glorious truth loomed ever larger: God
was their one and only source of strength, their one and
only hope, their one and only means of provision. He
alone stood between them and complete annihilation by
their powerful enemies. He had begun by teaching the
Israelites the lesson of faith, and then instructed them on
their duties to Himself and their fellowmen. Now came
the lesson that could only be learned by direct revelation
from God Himself—how to worship.

Since creation, man had searched for the ultimate
answers that would satisfy the desires of his heart and
soul. Though he had devised confusing and elaborate
schemes, the question still remained: What elements and
forms comprise the worship of God?

The latter part of the Book of Exodus (chapters
25—40) records the instructions for the construction of
the tabernacle. God spelled out the specifics:

- "Let them construct a sanctuary for Me, that I may dwell among them" (25:8)
- "They shall construct an ark" (25:10)
- "You shall make a mercy seat" (25:17)
- "Make two cherubim of gold" (25:17)
- "You shall set the bread of the Presence on the table before Me at all times" (25:30)
- "Make a lampstand of pure gold" (25:31)
- "Make its lamps seven" (25:37)

Many times God cautioned the Israelites to construct the tabernacle according to His directions. "See that you make them after the pattern for them, which was shown to you on the mountain" (25:40; see also 26:30).

The creation of the world must have been the most spectacular, awesome, and exciting demonstration of God's power ever known. Yet God describes it in one verse, "In the beginning God created the heaven and the earth" (Genesis 1:1, KJV).

In comparison, when the Israelites were told to construct the tabernacle, the detailed instructions were almost overwhelming. "And in the lampstand four cups shaped like almond blossoms, its bulbs and its flowers. And a bulb shall be under the first pair of branches coming out of it, and a bulb under the second pair of branches coming out of it, and a bulb under the third pair of branches coming out of it, for the six branches coming out of the lampstand. Their bulbs and their branches shall be of one piece with it; all of it shall be one piece of hammered work of pure gold" (Exodus 25:34-36). And the details continue chapter after chapter.

Why all this detail? Because worship is important to God. It is the means by which His Godhead is recognized and acknowledged. He ordained worship; He must also direct it. He will not accept any man-made schemes. Man must not enter into worship lightly or casually, for it is truly the most sacred exercise of the soul, the supreme human experience, his highest and noblest duty.

Day by day man can live to the glory of God. But there are also special times when the human spirit is borne along in adoration and praise. The daily walk with God and the special times of adoration combine in true worship of the Lord. Worship, then, is not merely an act, but a whole way of life.

WORSHIP IN THE DAILY GRIND

The table of showbread was an important feature of the tabernacle. Yet bread speaks of the ordinary things of life, the routines and the chores. God never allowed His people to forget that their worship included conducting their daily lives according to His will and to His glory.

Some years ago the Billy Graham organization sent out a plaque to be hung over the kitchen sink. It read: "Divine Services Conducted Here Daily." It was a simple reminder that even when we were doing dishes, we could do them unto the Lord. Worship is a way of life.

WORSHIP AND THE WORD OF GOD

The instructions concerning the tabernacle give great detail about the lampstand, which speaks of the Word of God. Lamp imagery is found throughout the Old Testament. "Thy Word is a lamp to my feet, and a light to my path" (Psalm 119:105). "The unfolding of Thy words gives light; it gives understanding to the simple" (Psalm 119:130). "The commandment is a lamp, and the teaching is light; and reproofs for discipline the way of life'' (Proverbs 6:23).

Some 200 years ago, Americans got together and wrote the document called the Constitution of the United States. By anybody's judgment, it is a remarkable work. Other nations have copied from it. Great statesmen of the world have marvelled at it. But do you know what you find at the end? Amendments! It needed improvement.

Many centuries before the American Constitution, God wrote the Law of the whole earth. Do you know what you find at the end of it? No amendments. Not even one. The Bible stands as written. The reason for this is simple: ''The law of the Lord is perfect, restoring the soul; the testimony of the Lord is sure, making wise the simple. The precepts of the Lord are right, rejoicing the heart; the commandment of the Lord is pure, enlightening the eyes. The fear of the Lord is clean, enduring forever; the judgments of the Lord are true; they are righteous altogether'' (Psalm 19:7-9). This marvelous Word of God should be a part of our daily worship—our daily way of life.

The Apostle Paul stated, ''All Scripture is given by inspiration of God, and is profitable for doctrine, for reproof, for correction, for instruction in righteousness; that the man of God may be perfect, thoroughly furnished unto all good works'' (2 Timothy 3:16-17, KJV). Three out of the four reasons why God gave us His Word relate to doing something with it—the direct application of the Word of God to our lives.

Doctrine: that's what we are to believe.

Reproof: that's what we are to stop doing. Some wrong practices die hard. After my arrival in Minneapolis to enroll in Northwestern College, I checked into a nearby hotel. Following my enrollment in the college—with a Bible major—I returned to the hotel. When I was ready to check out, I stuffed all the towels into my suitcase. I thought nothing of it at the time. Months later, as I was doing a personal Bible study, the Lord spoke directly and squarely to me about my stealing.

Correction: that's what we are to change or do better, and there are always many things in our lives that God wants us to improve.

Instruction in righteousness: that's what we are to continue doing to build ourselves up. Through Bible study, we learn what our lives ought to look like. I know people who would die rather than deny the inspiration of Scripture. But what is Scripture for? "That the man of God may be perfect, throughly furnished unto all good works" (2 Timothy 3:17, KJV). If I believe that, I will spend time in the Word. Sometimes the same man who would die for the inspiration of Scripture hardly ever opens his Bible. He misses the whole point. The Bible is given for our daily walk and should be part of our daily worship.

James uses an interesting phrase to describe the Word of God. "But the man who looks intently into the perfect law that gives freedom, and continues to do this, not forgetting what he has heard, but doing it—he will be blessed in what he does" (James 1:25). *The perfect law that gives freedom?* I don't know how it is with you, but I never associate law with liberty. Whenever I see a policeman, I slow down, no matter what speed I'm going. It's automatic. I nearly always associate law with restriction.

At first "the perfect law that gives freedom" seems to involve a contradiction of terms. A washing machine comes with certain instructions—amount of soap to use per load, the limits of pounds of laundry per load, and so on. Are these instructions meant to restrict you? No, they are meant for your good, that you might get the most trouble-free hours of use from the machine.

How about a prescription from your doctor? When you get it from the drugstore, the label reads, "One every four hours," or "Take two at meals and at bedtime." Why? Larger dosages could be harmful and smaller ones would not yield the maximum results. The amounts on the label are not meant to cause you hurt or consternation by their limitations; they are given to help you recover to full health.

So it is with most of life. Certain cleaning fluids under our sink have warnings on the labels. "Don't drink." "Don't breathe the fumes." "Don't get it into the eyes." Why not? The products are mine, aren't they? Can't I do as I please with them? Of course, but I'll be sorry if I misuse them. Daily living has its natural limitations.

God invented life and afterward He gave us a manual. We often say, "When all else fails, read the instructions." That's the point of the Bible. It was given to show us how to live, to give us a standard to follow.

Imagine coming up for a race. Everyone crouches at the starting line. Then someone says, "What race is this?" The starter answers, "I don't know."

"Is this the 40-yard dash or the cross-country race?"

"I don't know; no one said."

"Well, the way I start out depends on what it is."

"I don't know what it is."

"I see; which way is the tape?"

"I don't know."

What kind of race would that be?

We laugh, but there is a significant school of thought today that says that's the way the world is and that's the way your life should be lived. Your friends or children are hearing today that there are no absolutes. That's absolute nonsense. People err by following the wrong rules or no rules at all. God says, "Here they are, the standards that will work, laid out clear and plain." We then must choose whether or not to obey His guidelines.

WORSHIP AND EARNEST PRAYER

"Moreover, you shall set the gold altar of incense before the ark of the testimony, and set up the veil for the doorway to the tabernacle" (Exodus 40:5). Incense had to do with prayer. The Apostle John, in his vision of heaven, identified the incense as being "the prayers of the saints" (Revelation 5:8). Prayer is a vital part of a life-style of worship.

Prayer is also crucial in spiritual warfare. Before the wars of conquest in Canaan, Israel had to take on the Amalekites, who were strong and experienced (see Exodus 17). Joshua's forces, newly released from slavery, knew nothing of the strategy and tactics of warfare.

Humanly speaking, the outcome of the battle was obvious. Any Las Vegas gambler would have laid monumental odds on Amalek. But the battle was not to be won by human means. Moses, the man of God, stood on a high hill with a panoramic view of the entire battleground. "So it came about when Moses held his hand up, that Israel prevailed, and when he let his hand down, Amalek prevailed" (Exodus 17:11).

Moses quickly discovered that the outcome of the battle depended on prayer. "But Moses' hands were heavy. Then they took a stone and put it under him, and he sat on it; and Aaron and Hur supported his hands, one on one side and one on the other. Thus his hands were steady until the sun set. So Joshua overwhelmed Amalek and his people with the edge of the sword'' (Exodus 17:12-13). We must never forget this lesson in our own warfare of the Spirit. The battles of life are won by prayer. Prayer is the central factor in everything.

Lorne Sanny, president of The Navigators, teaches that prayer is not preparation for the work of God, but actually *is* the work of God. He has seen this in the expansion of the work worldwide. Many people incorrectly believe that the remarkable growth of The Navigators' ministry is simply a result of the careful application of certain principles. Although principles from God's Word shape our global plans, which are hammered out in consultation with world Christian leadership, the foundation of the work is diligent prayer.

In the 1930s, Dawson Trotman and a Christian friend spent 40 mornings in earnest prayer over a map of the world. They prayed over cities, countries, and continents, asking God to raise up a disciplemaking ministry. Today these prayers are being answered, both in the expansion of the Navigator ministry and in the quality of the results.

James wrote, ''The prayer of a righteous man is powerful and effective'' (James 5:16). Do the words *powerful* and *effective* describe your prayers?

When Saul of Tarsus was converted, God told Ananias that Saul was praying and to go heal his blind eyes (see Acts 9:10-12). For years Saul had said long, elaborate, flowery prayers. As a Pharisee, this was part of his religious duty. Now he was praying in his room, without sight and food. Imagine the picture in heaven. Gabriel and Michael, the archangels, are talking. Michael says, ''Hey, Saul of Tarsus is finally praying.''

Gabriel looks up and says, ''You mean, saying prayers, right?''

"No, I mean praying."

"Saul of Tarsus?"

"Yes."

So they both go over and look down. Sure enough, Saul is really praying for the first time in his life. As a Pharisee, he had said prayers for years, but now he had begun to pray.

Do you pray or do you say prayers?

WORSHIP AND TOTAL DEDICATION

"And you shall set the altar of burnt offering in front of the doorway of the tabernacle of the tent of meeting" (Exodus 40:6). Burnt offerings speak of total surrender, an offering of our lives on God's altar to be consumed in the flames of His love. That's what God desires.

The Apostle Paul taught that total dedication constituted worship. "Therefore, I urge you, brothers, in view of God's mercy, to offer yourselves as living sacrifices, holy and pleasing to God—*which is your spiritual worship*" (Romans 12:1).

One summer Virginia and I met a girl from Sweden. Ruth was a beautiful girl, completely dedicated to Jesus Christ. As she gave her testimony, she told us about praying over Romans 12:1-2 at a New Year's Eve service at her church. The minister had exhorted the people of the congregation to commit their bodies to God as best they knew how. Ruth did this, seriously committing each part of her body to the Lord. Several years later, a bus struck her and she lost one of her legs. Commenting on her loss, she smiled and said, "You really can't lose what you've already given away, can you?" She had committed her body to God.

We ask ourselves, "What am I doing with my life? Am I holding on to it for myself, or have I committed it to God?" Jesus said, "If anyone wants to follow in My footsteps, he must *give up all right to himself,* carry his cross every day and keep close behind Me" (Luke 9:23, PH). If we are serious about a life-style of worship, we must settle that issue.

What will that mean? It will mean a life lived for God's glory (see Romans 12:2). Self will no longer reign. Christ Himself will take His rightful place on the thrones of our hearts and we will learn the blessings of living to His glory. He will lead; we will follow. He will speak; we will listen. He will encourage us when we are down, soothe us when we hurt, and cheer us when we are sad. Such a life has no equal.

For the Apostle Peter, the issue of wholehearted dedication was settled early. Jesus had used Peter's boat as a rostrum from which to teach the people on shore. Then He told Peter and his partners to put out into deeper water and let down their nets for a catch.

Peter might have thought, *Look, You're a carpenter and I'm a fisherman, and I know that fish don't bite during the daytime. This lake gets so hot that you can cook an egg on it. Besides, my wife has my breakfast ready and you can't keep a woman waiting breakfast.*

What he actually said, however, was, "Master, we've worked hard all night and haven't caught anything. But because You say so, I will let down the nets" (Luke 5:5).

The fishermen had never done it before, but at Christ's word they would let down the nets. Faith needs no precedent. What happened as a result? They caught so many fish that both of their boats were filled to the point of sinking. I'm not a fisherman, but I know this: it takes a tremendous number of fish to sink a fishing boat.

Peter and his companions were astounded at this display of Christ's divinity. So Jesus said to Peter, "Don't be afraid; from now on you will catch men" (5:10).

What was their response? Did they say, "Lord, this is no time to quit the fishing business. You go ahead and preach and we'll stay here and support the work. We've been doing it wrong all our lives; we'll fish in the daytime"?

Instead of arguing, "they pulled their boats up on shore, left everything and followed Him" (5:11). The word *everything* should be underlined. They had finally hit the jackpot, after years of work. They had two large mountains of beautiful, silvery fish. They were professional fishermen who now had made it big.

But they left everything. There's a principle involved here, and it doesn't mean you have to get out of your present business (whatever it is). *The principle here is surrendering all to God*—your life, your possessions, your work, your family, whatever.

Contrast Peter's response with that of the rich young ruler (see Mark 10:17-22). Jesus told him, "Go, sell everything you have and give to the poor, and you will have treasure in heaven. Then come, follow Me" (10:21). The man looked at his stack of trinkets and then he looked at Jesus and back again. And he went away sorrowing, for he could not give them up.

Someone in the next generation—if the Lord tarries—may be grateful that you didn't forsake God. He may thank God for every memory of you because of the impact your life had on his. The exciting Christian life starts when you lay your life on the altar of God to be consumed by His love and to be used in His great cause.

Let nothing stand in the way of a total surrender of your life to God. A life lived for self gains small and puny results. But a life totally dedicated to God has the potential of doing momentous good—easing pain, helping others through life's tough battles, solving some of the perplexing ills of the world. The choice is yours: self or Christ. Go ahead. Take the plunge. "Then He spoke to them all: 'If anyone wants to follow in My footsteps, he must give up all right to himself, carry his cross every day and keep close behind Me' " (Luke 9:23, PH).

WORSHIP AND PURITY OF LIFE

"And you shall set the laver between the tent of meeting and the altar, and put water in it" (Exodus 40:7). The water-filled laver represents purity of life. A life of worship and service for Jesus Christ requires purity.

In preparation for the miraculous crossing of the Jordan River on dry ground and their entrance into Canaan, Joshua said to the people, "Consecrate yourselves, for tomorrow the Lord will do wonders among you" (Joshua 3:5). God was going to perform a miracle and He didn't want the people to miss the blessing. Today God is still doing wonders, and He doesn't want you to miss them. Sanctify yourself so that you'll be in on them, so that you'll see them, so that they will become part of your life and your daily worship of God.

The Prophet Jeremiah describes the converse of a godly person. "Cursed is the man who trusts in mankind and makes flesh his strength, and whose heart turns away from the Lord. For he will be like a bush in the desert, and will not see when prosperity comes, but will live in stony wastes in the wilderness, a land of salt without inhabitant" (Jeremiah 17:5-6).

What a shame to miss the reality of God's presence

and guidance completely. Why does it happen? Often because man's basic motivation is in the wrong direction. He lusts after and craves those things that are in direct opposition to the will of God. As he pursues them, he turns his back on the Lord, tunes his ears to the devil's lies, and fixes his eyes on the ambitions of the flesh. Evil grows in his mind and thoughts. In that condition, he will obviously miss the perfect plans and pleasant pastures of God.

The principle to remember is this: worship is a way of life. It is not just an act.

WORSHIP AND SEPARATION

"And you shall set up the court all around and hang up the veil for the gateway of the court" (Exodus 40:8). This veil, a separation between the tabernacle and the outer court, speaks to us of separation from the world. There are many powerful passages in the Bible on the subject of separation.

As Christians, we must keep one thing constantly in mind. We must carefully choose the company we keep. Scripture says, "He who walks with wise men will be wise, but the companion of fools will suffer harm" (Proverbs 13:20). David could say, "I am a companion of all those who fear Thee, and of those who keep Thy precepts" (Psalm 119:63).

Jesus Christ, a friend of publicans and sinners, was often their guest. His answer to criticism as to why He was eating with such people is very interesting. "The Son of Man came eating and drinking, and they say, 'Here is a glutton and a drunkard, a friend of tax collectors and "sinners." ' But wisdom is proved right by her actions"

(Matthew 11:19). *The New English Bible* renders that last sentence, "And yet God's wisdom is proved right by its results." It is obvious that if Jesus was looking for results, He must have had a goal. A person doesn't think in terms of results unless he has set out to try to accomplish something.

What was Jesus' objective, His goal? Jesus said, "For the Son of Man came to seek and to save what was lost" (Luke 19:10). That was His objective. Jesus ate with Zaccheus, the noted publican, because He wanted to seek him out and to save him.

I read that in ancient times you could tell where a person was going by the kind of questions he asked the innkeeper. If he asked, "Do you know of anyone who is traveling to London?" he was saying that he was going to London and would like to travel with someone else. In the same way, our destinations determine the kind of company we keep. Christians are strangers and pilgrims in the big inn of earth, and we're just stopping temporarily en route to heaven. In the inn, people can tell where we're going by the crowd we seek.

We have all been raised in the dominion of Satan, the god and spirit of this world who is working in the children of disobedience. We all got our start there, but somewhere along the way it occurred to us that we were no longer part of that crowd. That, for me, is a positive look at this whole business of separation from the world.

I am a companion of all those who love the Lord. That's why I love to attend church services. The church is a great leveller. When I go to church, I can get on my knees with the bank president, the janitor who cleans the bank, and another person who may never have been inside a bank. We're all together. What a wonderful experience. "The rich and poor meet together; the Lord is the

Maker of them all'' (Proverbs 22:2, KJV). Isn't that beautiful?

WORSHIP AND PUBLIC CONSECRATION

"Then you shall take the anointing oil and anoint the tabernacle and all that is in it, and shall consecrate it and all its furnishings; and it shall be holy. And you shall anoint the altar of burnt offering and all its utensils, and consecrate the altar; and the altar shall be most holy. And you shall anoint the laver and its stand, and consecrate it" (Exodus 40:9-11). In other words, when the Israelites finally completed the tabernacle, they publicly dedicated everything to God.

Such dedication is also a living, vital part of worship. Everything that we are and have—our families, our businesses, our lives—should be dedicated to God. If you've never actually done that, do it now. It will be the beginning of a new life with Jesus Christ as Lord of all.

TOPICS FOR STUDY

1. The New Testament's teaching on worship (topical study).
2. Worship in the Tabernacle and Temple (Old Testament).
3. Write out a public worship service, using only the Bible, supporting what you have in it with Scripture.
4. Worship in the Book of Hebrews.
5. Worship in the Book of Revelation.
6. The importance of the object of worship in worship.

APPLICATION: On the basis of this chapter, how can I worship better and more biblically in the future? Write out what you are going to do.

CHAPTER FIVE

THE MOST IMPORTANT ELEMENT
The Lesson in Obedience

Study Material: Exodus 32; Deuteronomy 9; Psalm 106; Jeremiah 33; Ezekiel 14; Acts 7; 1 Corinthians 10

YOU look at what the Israelites did and it overwhelms you. How could they do such a stupid thing? Would anyone trade all the oil in the Middle East for a lollipop? Would anyone trade heaven for hell? No one would be so foolish. Yet Israel, whom the Lord had led and encouraged and nourished for some months, traded their glorious, eternal, loving God for a calf.

"Oh, come now—a calf!" you may exclaim.

That's right. They transferred their allegiance from God to a calf, something fashioned by their own hands.

"Impossible!" you say.

Unfortunately and tragically, it is true. Through this unbelievable incident, however, the Lord taught His people one more dramatic, powerful lesson: the necessity of obedience.

While all the instructions for worship discussed in chapter 4 were being given (Exodus 25—40), Moses was up on Mount Sinai with God, receiving the two tables of testimony—the tables of Law written with the finger of God.

Then tragedy occurred. "Now when the people saw that Moses delayed to come down from the mountain, the people assembled about Aaron, and said to him, 'Come, make us a god who will go before us; as for this Moses, the man who brought us up from the land of Egypt, we do not know what has become of him' '' (Exodus 32:1).

WHY DO PEOPLE DISOBEY GOD?

"Come, make us a god." There were two reasons for this particular disobedience. One was the prolonged absence of Moses, who had gone up the mountain with the consent of the people (see Exodus 20:18-19). For 39 days he had been communing with God in the mount. But he was away, and "when the cat is away, the mice will play." Jesus spoke of that, "When He saw the crowds, He had compassion on them, because they were harassed and helpless, like sheep without a shepherd" (Matthew 9:36). People do need leadership.

If you know much about sheep, you know that being called sheep is not very flattering. Years ago the people forming the Detroit major league baseball team were looking for a name. If someone had suggested the Detroit Sheep, how would that have gone over? No way. They wanted Tigers—claws, teeth, ferocity. Some years later a football team was organized. Suppose someone again suggested the Detroit Sheep. Still no good. This time the officials decided on the Detroit Lions—claws, teeth, ferocity again. I don't know of any athletic team anywhere called the "sheep." Nobody wants to be known as sheep. But people are sheep-like and tend to go astray without proper shepherding.

The second and most basic reason that the Israelites went back to idolatry can be traced back to Egypt. They had never gotten their lust for Egyptian idolatry out of their systems. Ezekiel writes, "Nor did they forsake the idols of Egypt" (Ezekiel 20:8). Stephen revealed their root problem when he declared, "In their hearts [they] turned back to Egypt" (Acts 7:39). They were looking back, lusting after the idols of Egypt.

With Moses gone, they wanted a new god. Was Moses their god? Had God deserted them? No, Moses was only their leader. So logically what they should have asked for was a new leader, not a new god. But caught up in their lust for sin, they did not think clearly.

Notice what they wanted: a god that would go before them (Exodus 32:1). They wanted to make a god with their own hands, one that they could carry with their own hands, one who would go when they wanted to, stop when they desired, turn right or left when they wished. They wanted a god that would do their bidding. In our saner moments we never want that, but from time to time we may find ourselves falling into the same mentality.

WHY DO CHRISTIAN LEADERS DISOBEY GOD?

Aaron's response to Israel's request for a new god is indeed disturbing. "Tear off the gold rings which are in the ears of your wives, your sons, and your daughters, and bring them to me" (Exodus 32:2). There is a lot of speculation as to why Aaron said this. He may have said it to try to put off the people. He must have thought, *You want a new god? Oh, sick. What am I going to do? Moses isn't here. Ah, I'll put them off. I'll make the price so high that they will forget it. They aren't going to want to strip off all their jewelry.*

So he told them and they said, "Great!" Aaron forgot that people will pay to sin. He made the same mistake we often make; he tried to trick the devil. But the devil—the master of deceit and father of lies—is filled with all guile and falsehood. Since we cannot trick him, we must resist him (see James 4:7).

Let's imagine what Moses would have done if he had been there.

"Moses?" the people would have called.

"Yes?"

"We'd like to have a new god."

"A new *what?* Are you out of your minds? NO!"

"Oh! Well, we just thought we'd ask. Sorry we brought it up."

One good resounding "no" could have settled the whole thing right at that point. But Aaron made a tactical error and the people fell when Moses had only one more day up on the mountain.

WHY DOES DISOBEDIENCE CONTINUE?

"Then all the people tore off the gold rings which were in their ears, and brought them to Aaron. And he took this from their hand, and fashioned it with a graving tool, and made it into a molten calf; and they said, 'This is your god, O Israel, who brought you up from the land of Egypt.' Now when Aaron saw this, he built an altar before it; and Aaron made proclamation and said, 'Tomorrow shall be a feast to the Lord' " (Exodus 32:3-5).

Sin is always self-perpetuating. You fall in love with an idol, build an altar to it, then find yourself back at that altar tomorrow and all of your tomorrows thereafter.

The world contains multitudes of such shrines and idols. Each requires a sacrifice. Each has before it an altar on which your gifts are to be laid. Often they can be very subtle. They are not inherently evil, but are idols only because they demand a supreme loyalty to themselves. This can be the case with pleasure, knowledge, recreation, or any number of things.

If you love money, for example, pretty soon you will be at the altar of money every day. Millions make such daily pilgrimages to the god of wealth and riches. Only after years of faithful worship do they discover the awful truth. Money does not satisfy. It cannot, because no matter how much you get, you always need a little bit more. Other idols are the lazy, comfortable figure called the love of ease and the strong and vigorous one called fame.

Men of the world labor to tend their idol altars. Life becomes a constant burden. The more one lays on the altar, the more is demanded. Life becomes torn between the constant demands of the various idols of the soul. Each idol seems to demand an isolated loyalty to itself. And what is the ultimate result? "What benefit did you reap at that time [before you were Christians] from the things you are now ashamed of? Those things result in death!" (Romans 6:21)

The immediate result of Israel's sin was not death but gaiety. "And the people sat down to eat and to drink, and rose up to play" (Exodus 32:6). They no doubt thought they were having a great time with their new god. It doesn't say they rose up to labor or they rose up to become more holy, but they rose up to play. It was great fun and games, but with what result?

The Apostle Paul gives us a divine summary, "Nevertheless, God was not pleased with most of them, so their bodies were scattered over the desert. Now these things occurred as examples, to keep us from setting our hearts on evil things as they did" (1 Corinthians 10:5-6).

The very first specific example Paul then cited was this golden calf incident. "Do not be idolaters, as some of them were; as it is written: 'The people sat down to eat and drink and got up to indulge in pagan revelry' " (10:7).

Of course, Moses, up on the mountain, knew nothing about the people's sin until God revealed it to him. "Then the Lord spoke to Moses, 'Go down at once, for your people, whom you brought up from the land of Egypt, have corrupted themselves. They have quickly turned aside from the way which I commanded them' " (Exodus 32:7-8). That is just what sin does. It corrupts us and it turns us aside from the way of God.

DISOBEDIENCE AND INTERCESSION

After alerting Moses to what the people had done, God said, "Now then let Me alone, that My anger may burn against them, and that I may destroy them; and I will make of you a great nation" (Exodus 32:10).

This passage contains one of the most dramatic statements on the power of intercessory prayer to be found in the entire Bible. God said to Moses, "Let Me alone." He said, in effect, "I know what happens when you start praying. So don't get on your knees now, just let Me alone." When God's decree goes forth, nothing will stop it, but it had not yet been given.

We have examples of situations in which it is too late for intercession. "Then the word of the Lord came to me saying, 'Son of man, if a country sins against Me by committing unfaithfulness, and I stretch out My hand against it, destroy its supply of bread, send famine against it, and cut off from it both man and beast, even though these three men, Noah, Daniel, and Job were in its midst,

by their own righteousness they could only deliver themselves,' declares the Lord God" (Ezekiel 14:12-14).

God also said to Jeremiah, "Even though Moses and
Samuel were to stand before Me, My heart would not be
with this people; send them away from My presence and
let them go!" (Jeremiah 15:1) In these cases, God's decree
had already gone forth. In the passage before us now, it
had not. Can you imagine what Moses was thinking? *The
people are down there sinning; God's name is blasphemed; tremendous trouble is brewing*. In the midst of all
this, God gave Moses a test.

God sometimes tests us when we least expect it.
What's the best kind of test to give, to find out if the people
really know the material? A pop quiz. This is what God
did. He said in effect, "I'm going to found a whole new
race of people and you're going to be the new head—the
founder, the director, the top man. So I want you to leave
this group you're with now, and I'm going to make you top
man of the Mosesites."

When God said to Moses, *"Your people . . .* have
corrupted themselves" (Exodus 32:7), Moses had
replied,"Lord, why doth Thine anger burn against *Thy
people* whom Thou has brought out from the land of Egypt
with great power and with a might hand?" (32:11) Nobody
wanted to claim these people at this point.

In spite of this, Moses did a remarkable thing. He put
the salvation of these people above his own name and
prestige. Once again he proved that he was a tremendous
leader. The psalmist wrote, "Therefore He said that He
would destroy them, had not Moses His chosen one stood
in the breach before Him, to turn away His wrath from
destroying them" (Psalm 106:23). This is fantastic
power—the power of intercessory prayer.

Toward the end of their training in the wilderness,

when Israel was ready to enter into Canaan, the people were reminded what all this had been about. "Remember, do not forget how you provoked the Lord your God to wrath in the wilderness; from the day that you left the land of Egypt until you arrived at this place, you have been rebellious against the Lord. Even at Horeb you provoked the Lord to wrath, and the Lord was so angry with you that He would have destroyed you . . . . And I fell down before the Lord, as at the first, forty days and nights; I neither ate bread nor drank water, because of all your sin which you had committed in doing what was evil in the sight of the Lord to provoke Him to anger. For I was afraid of the anger and hot displeasure with which the Lord was wrathful against you in order to destroy you, but the Lord listened to me that time also" (Deuteronomy 9:7-8, 18-19).

The fact that God had not destroyed them on the spot was a miracle of mercy. If God had dealt with them on the basis of what they deserved, they would have perished then and there. You and I can look at each other and nod assent. We know our merits cannot justify us in the eyes of God, for our works condemn us. In the instance with the golden calf, the sin was committed in the very place where the Law was given which expressly forbade the worship of images. While Moses was away receiving the tablets of stone, while the mount still glowed with smoke and fire, the people quickly left the ways of God. They surely must have realized their narrow escape as they later observed Moses fasting and beseeching God for 40 days on their behalf.

God invites us to benefit from the great blessing of answered prayer as well. "Call to Me . . . and I will answer you, and I will tell you great and mighty things, which you do not know" (Jeremiah 33:3).

What keeps us from the throne of grace? Probably

different things with different people. For some it might be a problem with priorities. We just don't put first things first. We major on the minors. Or we think that by scheming or manipulating, rather than praying, we will accomplish our goals without having to pray.

Some people doubt the power of prayer. They are just not convinced of what Jesus said, "I will do whatever you ask in My name, so that the Son may bring glory to the Father. You may ask Me for anything in My name, and I will do it" (John 14:13-14).

One problem is common to us all. Our sinful, corrupted flesh cringes and rebels at the idea of spending time in the presence of a Holy God. As we invest time with Him, we become more aware of our own lustful ambitions and pride, and that's hard on us. So we avoid it. We busy ourselves with other good things while neglecting the best. But when we do pray—earnestly and fervently—we come away with the glow of God on our souls.

What was the content of Moses' intercession? What reasons did he give God for not destroying Israel? He began by asking this interesting question: "Lord, why doth Thine anger burn?" (Exodus 32:11) The Israelites were, in fact, unworthy to be delivered from Egypt in the first place. They didn't deserve it; they were idolaters in Egypt just as they were now. But they were God's people nevertheless. Moses was saying, "Lord, remember Your unique relationship with these people."

Actually, Moses was pleading three things. First he said, "If You do what You intend, all that has gone before will be fruitless. Remember when You exercised Your strong hand in delivering the people from Egypt? Remember when You rolled back the Red Sea and took them safely across? These great acts of deliverance will lose their luster if You destroy the people now."

Second, Moses was concerned for the glory of God's great name. Israel was dear to Moses, but so was God's testimony among the nations. He could not bear to have the Egyptians mocking his Lord (see Exodus 32:12). The eyes of the neighboring nations were on Israel. What happened to them would reflect on God. His enemies would contend that God brought the people out, not to sacrifice to the Lord, but to be sacrificed by Him.

Third, Moses reminded God that the promises He had made to Abraham, Isaac, and Jacob would go unfulfilled (see Exodus 32:13). If Israel was cut off, what would become of the eternal promises He had made? Admittedly, the Israelites had disobeyed and acted in unbelief. Should their disobedience and unbelief make God's promises void? God forbid!

God's promises are also to be the basis for our prayers. Here's a very interesting thing: the promises of God prompt our prayers, then prayer activates the promises of God. As you go through the Word and see a promise from God, it should so excite you that you'll stop, get on your knees, and begin to pray about it. Then prayer will activate the promise in your life. That's what happened to Moses.

As a result of his prayers, "the Lord changed His mind about the harm which He said He would do to His people" (32:14). God pressed ahead with His punishment for their sin but did not destroy them. They needed to be punished, so that they might learn a lesson about the dangers of disobedience. Nevertheless, the compassion of God once again shone through. How ready He was to forgive! The lesson is plain. He not only pardons those who repent; He hears and heeds the intercession of others.

During the 1960s, thousands of young nomads roamed the United States. They wandered aimlessly from coast to coast, searching for fulfillment, kicks, or "reality," and turned to drugs and immorality. The problem was that they were looking in the wrong direction. They were generally in rebellion against the "establishment"—its religion, middle class values, and other cultural mores. In order to share Christ's better way with them, The Navigators established a summer ministry in Boulder, Colorado, one of their favorite stopping-off points on the road east or west.

We met hundreds of them. They came in all shapes and sizes. Searching. Cynical. Uptight. Rebellious. Depressed. Fearful. The overriding fact that stands out above all others in looking back on those days is this: sin had corrupted them, turning them from the only path that could lead to the satisfaction, peace, and joy they craved (see Exodus 32:7-8). That's what sin does in our lives; it corrupts us and turns us aside from the ways of God.

To our surprise (which is to our shame), scores of those young people were ready to turn to Christ. We saw Him restore lives that had been corrupted with sin and put them on the path of righteousness. That which sin had fouled became a thing of beauty.

THE DRASTIC RESULTS OF DISOBEDIENCE

Then Moses went down to rejoin the people and it was his turn to become angry. He had pleaded with God not to burn with anger but when he actually saw what the people had done, "Moses' anger burned, and he threw the tablets from his hands and shattered them at the foot of the mountain" (Exodus 32:19). There is a lot of speculation as to why Moses did this. Did he sin?

In all likelihood, Moses was trying to get across to the

people the gravity and greatness of their sin. They had made an idol and had given themselves to pagan revelry. Moses had to do something to display how desperate their situation really was. White shows up best on a dark background; often it takes something drastic to make people realize what they have done.

By appearing suddenly and breaking the stone tablets, Moses no doubt stunned the people. He showed graphically what they had done. His act of breaking the tablets was a visual aid that God's covenant with them was broken. It also drove home the point vividly, and created memories which would stick in their minds for a long time to come.

What had Israel done? They had sinned, of course, but there was more. They had not only abandoned God for a calf; they had broken their covenant with Him. The people had agreed to this covenant in a solemn ceremony. "Then he took the Book of the Covenant and read it in the hearing of the people; and they said, 'All that the Lord has spoken we will do, and we will be obedient!' So Moses took the blood and sprinkled it on the people, and said, 'Behold, the blood of the covenant, which the Lord has made with you in accordance with all these words' " (Exodus 24:7-8).

Then Moses "took the calf which they had made and burned it with fire, and ground it to powder, and scattered it over the surface of the water, and made the sons of Israel drink it" (32:20). Can you imagine that? Many people feel that Aaron went along with the people's idolatry because he was afraid of what they might do to him. At that stage of the game, it was about 2,000,000 to one. Moses, however, didn't fear the people; he feared God. He showed them how powerless this god of theirs really was. With the boldness of God burning in his spirit, he made the people drink their pulverized idol. The greatest antidote for the fear of man is the fear of God.

The next item on Moses' agenda was to deal with Aaron. "What did this people do to you, that you have brought such great sin upon them?" Moses demanded (32:21).

Aaron's reply comes across as one of the weakest excuses ever offered. "I threw it [the gold] into the fire and out came this calf" (32:24). He was saying, "I didn't have anything to do with this. Boy! Was I surprised when that calf came out. You could have knocked me over with a feather." No one likes to claim the results of sin, so Aaron tried to get off the hook. And our excuses for sin often ring as hollow to the ears of God as Aaron's does to us.

"Then Moses stood in the gate of the camp and said, 'Whoever is for the Lord, come to me!' And all the sons of Levi gathered together to him" (32:26). A word of caution: we're getting into a tough part of Scripture at this point. Remember this: what happens next would not have had to happen, because Moses said, "Whoever is for the Lord, come to me!"

"And he said to them, 'Thus says the Lord, the God of Israel, "Every man of you put his sword upon his thigh, and go back and forth from gate to gate in the camp, and kill every man his brother, and every man his friend, and every man his neighbor." ' So the sons of Levi did as Moses instructed, and about three thousand men of the people fell that day" (32:27-28).

Aaron had no idea that his actions would lead to the death of 3,000 men. We, too, have the option to do anything we please, but we cannot control the consequences of our actions. We may break the law, but somebody else will determine the results.

As you go along in life, you'll face an option which won't appear to be much at all. The option will be either to do right or wrong. You may think, *Oh, well, this isn't such a big deal.* Quite often, however, the consequences of your choice are far greater than the decision itself. To illustrate, an earthquake in Alaska may do only minor damage—a few old buildings due to come down anyway may suffer and there may be no loss of life. That earthquake, however, may trigger a tidal wave that sweeps across the ocean, devastating ships and islands in its path. The decision to act itself may seem minor, but the results down the line can be catastrophic.

The Exodus record does not tell us how God may have punished Aaron for his sin, but Scripture elsewhere leaves no doubt as to how God viewed it. Moses said, concerning this situation, "And the Lord was angry enough with Aaron to destroy him; so I also prayed for Aaron at the same time" (Deuteronomy 9:20).

It is vitally important for the Christian to make a basic commitment to be obedient to God, for he never knows what will result from disobedience. Lot didn't know the consequences of pitching his tent toward Sodom. As a result of the destruction of that city, he lost his wife, his sons-in-law, his home, his goods, and his self-respect.

THE CONCLUSION OF THE MATTER

After Moses had destroyed the golden calf, he went back up into the mountain to pray. "Then Moses returned to the Lord, and said, 'Alas, this people has committed a great sin, and they have made a god of gold for themselves. But now, if Thou wilt, forgive their sin—and if not, please blot me out from Thy book which Thou has written!' '' (Exodus 32:31-32) Note the dash after the word *sin*. I think that dash represents the point in Moses' prayer when he broke down and began to weep. I believe he lost all control at that point and began to sob before God.

On the surface, Moses seemed hard, tough, mean. To the people, it seemed like Moses didn't have much love for them. But they didn't know what was going on behind the scenes. Quite often a leader must have two faces. (I'm saying this in the right sense.) He does what he has to do and then weeps when he is alone with God.

How great was Moses' compassion for the people? Remember that he knew more about the glories of heaven than any other human being alive at that time. He had been in the actual presence of Almighty God in sweet communion. Yet he said, "God, if it will mean the salvation of these people, I am willing to have You blot my name out of the book. I am willing to be accursed from You." That's a powerful love.

For those who ask the meaning of the term *fervent prayer,* this is an example. It's not saying prayers, but praying, Moses was crying to God for the salvation of his people. The burden was so heavy on his heart that he was willing to sacrifice himself to atone for their sin.

This kind of prayer does not come to us quickly and easily. A strong prayer life has to be built on strong prayer legs. It's a matter of growth and development, So continue to plug away, with the goal to grow in the Lord. Have your quiet time, memorize the Word, meditate in the Scriptures. God may make you a prayer warrior, an unusual and powerful force in the cause of Christ.

The people were spared through the prayers of Moses even though their disobedience was punished. It is noteworthy that during the time when God was organizing the worship of Himself, He provided this lesson in obedience. Disobedience brought Israel to the very brink of disaster and, when all was said and done, they realized it. The words of the covenant they had ratified with God surely took on new meaning.

It is interesting to note that Moses first gave the covenant to the people verbally and they agreed to it. But then we read, "Moses wrote down all the words of the Lord" (Exodus 24:4). As soon as the Lord had made His covenant with His people, it became a written word by which He could govern them.

God has followed the same practice ever since. It is that way today and will be as long as the world stands. You and I must take heed to this tremendous truth. God's Word is our guide. There is no other. May God give us grace to learn His Word and, by the enlightenment and help of the Holy Spirit, apply its truths to our daily lives. God's promises and commands are given with our well-being in mind. The more we study them, the more reasons we shall see to walk with our God in joyful obedience.

TOPICS FOR STUDY

1. The New Testament concept of obedience.
2. The relationship of love and obedience. (We obey because we love God as a response to His love.)
3. Examples of obedience and disobedience in the Scriptures and their consequences.
4. The obedience of Jesus Christ to His Father.
5. The place of obedience in the Sinaitic Covenant (Exodus; Deuteronomy).
6. Obedience to leadership.

APPLICATION: What aspects of obedience do I need to apply to my life now? Write out what you will start doing immediately in this area.

CHAPTER SIX

VALIANT IN THE FIGHT
The Lesson in Courage

*Study Material: Numbers 13—14; Joshua 1; 2:9-11; 2 Kings
6; Acts 12; 2 Timothy 2:7-13; 4:6-8; Hebrews 3:10-11*

FEAR is one of the besetting problems of mankind.
Everywhere we turn we find men fearful—afraid of
starvation, death, the future, economic collapse, nearly
everything. Fear can be very disabling. That is why, in the
early days of World War II, President Franklin Delano
Roosevelt of the United States said, "The only thing we
have to fear is fear itself."

The Prophet Isaiah many centuries earlier warned the
people of Israel, "You are not to fear what they fear or be
in dread of it" (Isaiah 8:12). It is so easy to "catch" fear.
We have a tendency to let fear spread like an epidemic,
and to be seized by fear we see in others.

I know a person who was in a tornado once. It must
have been a dreadful experience, because after that if the
sky began to turn black, he would go into panic. Others
living in the same area never gave an anxious thought to a
mounting storm until this person began to talk about it and
utter dire predictions. Then *they* also became fearful. He
spread his fear to others. People who had experienced
hundreds of summer thunderstorms began to hunt for
shelters, convinced a tornado was on the way whenever
the sky grew dark.

Throughout history, people in difficulty or embarking on new ventures have needed great courage to cope with threats—whether real or imagined. Since the children of Israel were to face strong opposition in the conquest of the Promised Land, God had to teach them a lesson in courage. Note, for example, what God would later say to Joshua prior to his leading a new generation into the Promised Land—three times He would say, "Be strong and courageous" (Joshua 1:6-7, 9). The lesson, however, was to be a hard one. The Israelites would lose 40 years and a whole generation in learning it. But it was a necessary lesson, and in their case a necessary price.

What is the basis of godly strength and courage? God Himself. We are to be strong "in the Lord." Our courage is to be based on His promises. Joshua's courage did not have its roots in his own military genius but in the fact of God's presence and guidance. "No man will be able to stand before you all the days of your life. Just as I have been with Moses, I will be with you; I will not fail you or forsake you" (Joshua 1:5).

NEEDED: COURAGEOUS LEADERS

Our study in courage focuses on the expedition of the 12 spies whom Moses sent into the Promised Land some 38 years before the actual conquest under Joshua. "Then the Lord spoke to Moses saying, 'Send out for yourself men so that they may spy out the land of Canaan, which I am going to give to the sons of Israel; you shall send a man from each of their fathers' tribes, every one a leader among them' " (Numbers 13:1-3).

God had a purpose in selecting leaders. These were not draftees from among the ordinary people or volunteers for a hazardous mission. Only experienced leaders could teach courage. As they would go, the people would follow. Thus the lesson had to be learned by the leaders first.

Chief Crazy Horse was one of the great leaders of the Sioux Indians in the early days of the American West. He was a remarkable military strategist and tactician. Early in his youth, one of the elders of the tribe had prophesied that he would never be killed in battle. Crazy Horse believed the old man, and his heroics are legendary. He was absolutely fearless in a fight. His bold courage had an electric effect on other young braves in the tribe. They were inspired when he plunged fearlessly into the fray, and followed wherever he led.

This principle holds true in every phase of life. The Apostle Paul said, "Because of my chains, most of the brothers in the Lord have been encouraged to speak the Word of God more courageously and fearlessly" (Philippians 1:14). When other Christians saw Paul's bold testimony in the prison, it challenged them to a more courageous ministry for the Lord. Paul was a good and bold leader.

NEEDED: COMMON SENSE

"When Moses sent [the 12 men] to spy out the land of Canaan, he said to them, 'Go up there into the Negev; then go up into the hill country. And see what the land is like, and whether the people who live in it are strong or weak, whether they are few or many. And how is the land in which they live, is it good or bad? And how are the cities in which they live, are they like open camps or with fortifications? And how is the land, is it fat or lean? Are there trees in it or not? Make an effort then to get some of the fruit of the land' " (Numbers 13:17-20).

Some people think that Moses made a mistake. They believe he went beyond what God had commanded him to do. God had already given the Israelites the land, and his request for intelligence information was a reliance on the arm of the flesh. But that was not so. God wants us to claim His promises and trust His Word, but that does not mean that we are to toss common sense out the window. What Moses asked the spies to do was practical; it was common sense to go in and look things over and report back.

Solomon said, "Trust in the Lord with all your heart, and do not lean on your own understanding. In all your ways acknowledge Him, and He will make your paths straight" (Proverbs 3:5-6). He did not say that we are not to use our understanding; we are simply not to lean on it, not to depend wholly on it apart from God. Obviously we must depend on God at all times for all things. We know that to lean strictly on our own human reason would be to lean on a broken reed. It would fail us and we would fall.

Dawson Trotman used to encourage Navigator men and women to think and to use their minds. He would tell them, "Think! You can do a lot more than you realize."

He used to quote a friend of his in the business world who told him, "I can find men who can do everything but think and do things in the order of their importance."

Daws used to conduct seminars for us on how to think. To someone uncertain about what to do, he would say, "God gave you a lot of leading when He gave you a mind. Use it!" Along with such admonitions, he would challenge us to saturate our hearts, minds, and lives with the Word of God in order that we might learn to think God's thoughts after Him.

It was his prayer that through consistent Scripture memory, the Word of God would become lodged within us as the decisive influence of life, the effect of which would be diffused throughout our total personalities. On the one hand, he urged us to use our heads, learn to think, and develop our minds. But he always balanced those principles with the strong admonition to let the Word of God dwell in us richly, in all wisdom. We must use our minds, but rely on God's wisdom.

We have a beautiful illustration of this in the New Testament. Because of King Herod's hatred for Christians and his desire to ingratiate himself with the people, he imprisoned Peter. To make sure Peter did not escape, Herod surrounded him with 16 guards in the dungeon (see Acts 12:3-6). Then an angel came along, released Peter, and out they went—through all the gates, past all the guards, into the street.

As soon as the angel left him, Peter walked to the house where the church was praying for his release. After they finally let him in and he had given his testimony and talked with them for a while, he said in effect, "Now I'm going to get out of here and go hide where nobody can find me" (see 12:12-17).

Peter had been delivered in a miraculous way by the angel of God. He could very easily have said, "I'll stay here at the house, and when the soldiers come to the door, I'll open it and become invisible. I'll just trust God for another miracle." But Peter knew better than that. Though God had delivered him in a miraculous way, he now needed to use his common sense and go into hiding.

That is precisely what Moses did when he gave the spies the intelligence-gathering assignment. When they returned, they not only gave a glowing description of the land, but brought impressive evidence—a cluster of

grapes so large it was borne on a staff between two men
(see Numbers 13:21-27).

NEEDED: GOD'S PERSPECTIVE

The report of the spies concluded on a negative note. They
said, "Nevertheless, the people who live in the land are
strong, and the cities are fortified and very large; and
moreover we saw the descendants of Anak there. Amalek
is living in the land of the Negev and the Hittites and the
Jebusites and the Amorites are living in the hill country,
and the Canaanites are living by the sea and by the side of
the Jordan" (13:28-29).

Research into each of these tribes in a Bible dictionary
provides a description of these people. They were a
tough-looking assortment. The children of Anak were a
race of giants who had terrorized the children of Israel.
The Amalekites were a group of bedouins whom Israel
had defeated in their first battle after leaving Egypt. The
Hittites were a fierce-looking race with yellow skin, black
hair and eyes, receding foreheads, and protruding jaws.
The Jebusites were a warlike people, part of the Canaanites, with their headquarters at Jerusalem. The Amorites
were mountaineers—tall, fair-skinned, and blue-eyed.
The Canaanites were lowlanders who lived along the
Mediterranean Sea and the Jordan River valley.

A variety of people, obstacles, and problems opposed
Israel. Obviously no one set plan, no magic formula, no
standard operating procedure could be worked out ahead
of time and repeated time and again in their conquest of
the land. Each situation would be different and the Lord
would need to provide an amazing array of battle tactics
and strategies for victory.

"Then Caleb quieted the people before Moses, and said, 'We should by all means go up and take possession of it, for we shall surely overcome it' " (13:30). Notice that Caleb did not say conquer the land, but "take possession" of it. This shows how he thought. He trusted the power and the promises of God. He was ready to possess what God had already given them. The place was as good as conquered; it was their land. Tremendous! His stirring challenge was not prompted by the energy of the flesh but by the Holy Spirit. It was a ringing statement of faith. God has promised! Why sit around? Let's go!

Now that's leadership in the true sense of the term. He was not trying to get them to charge off into battle relying on their own strengths and abilities. His confidence was squarely in God, and he tried to turn the eyes of the people to the Lord. His faith was the bedrock on which his courage was based. He was ready to lead them into battle, ready to stake his life on the fact that God's promises were true.

So it should be with us. Our victory has been won by Jesus Christ on the cross. "But thanks be to God! He gives us the victory through our Lord Jesus Christ" (1 Corinthians 15:57). You and I do not have to struggle, plead, or hope for victory over our enemies, besetting sins, doubts, or whatever. Jesus is our victory. He is our freedom, our wisdom, our strength, our all in all.

"But the men who had gone up with [Caleb] said, 'We are not able to go up against the people, for they are too strong for us' " (Numbers 13:31). There are two very important words in that verse. "*We* are not able . . . they are too strong for *us*." Where were their minds? On themselves.

If you want to launch into spiritual defeat, get your mind on yourself. Of course "*we* are not able." *We* never have been. *We* are not able to provide for our own salvation. *We* are not able to understand the Scriptures apart from the Holy Spirit. *We* are not able to fight the good fight of faith apart from the Lord's strength. *We* are not able to do the will of God apart from the Word of God. When it comes right down to it, we are totally dependent people who must rely completely on the goodness and guidance of God.

What they were forgetting is that *God is able*. He had given them promises, but they had lost sight of them. Christians so often complain about how weak they are. That really doesn't have anything to do with anything. It's irrelevant. What does the Bible teach? "In quietness and trust is your strength" (Isaiah 30:15).

What was the real issue? Hundreds of years before, God had made a covenant with Abraham: "To your descendants I have given this land" (Genesis 15:18). Was God with them or not? He had demonstrated that He was. Did He not go before them? Yes, by a pillar of cloud by day and a pillar of fire by night. Was anything too hard for God? Of course not. Were the cities walled clear up to heaven so that even God couldn't see over? No. The issue was God and His promises. Would they believe Him or not?

Scripture sums up the majority report of the spies as follows: "So they gave out to the sons of Israel a bad report of the land which they had spied out, saying, 'The land through which we have gone, in spying it out, is a land that devours its inhabitants; and all the people whom we saw in it are men of great size' " (Numbers 13:32).

Years later the psalmist clarified the issue. "Then they despised the pleasant land; they did not believe in His Word" (Psalm 106:24).

Courage is not hiding your head in the sand and pretending that nothing is wrong. Courage acknowledges difficulties, but also believes in God. Courage acknowledges difficulties, but does not dwell on them. The 10 spies saw the obstacles, but were blind to God. That's the sure path to defeat.

In another setting, the servant of the Prophet Elisha saw a great host of the enemy and was terrified. "When the attendant of the man of God had risen early and gone out, behold, an army with horses and chariots was circling the city. And his servant said to him, 'Alas, my master! What shall we do?' " (2 Kings 6:15) Elisha permitted his servant to see the opposing force as it really was.

Then Elisha told him, " 'Do not fear, for those who are with us are more than those who are with them.' Then Elisha prayed and said, 'O Lord, I pray open his eyes, that he may see.' And the Lord opened the servant's eyes, and he saw; and behold, the mountain was full of horses and chariots of fire all around Elisha" (2 Kings 6:16-17).

God was still in control. All was not lost. By human eyesight, reason, and logic they did not have a chance. But there was more to their situation than met the eye.

That perception was the basic difference between the minority and majority reports. The 10 reasoned on a human level. Caleb and Joshua saw the same things they saw, but through the eyes of those whose hearts were fixed on the promises of God. If all we see and acknowledge are the problems before us and our own weaknesses and lack of wisdom, we are defeated before we start. But God can give us the courage to press ahead if we turn to Him by faith.

During a plane flight, I was seated next to a nun, a Sister of Mercy. She asked if I would like to read part of her newspaper. In it was an interview with Congressional Medal of Honor recipients. Asked to define courage, they all answered that courage is doing the things you're afraid of. It is not lack of fear. Acknowledging our difficulties may make us afraid, but trusting God gives us courage to go forward anyhow.

To use an illustration, a giant might stand about 84 inches high and a dwarf about 48 inches. That's a difference of 36 inches. Viewed from ground level that would appear to be quite significant, but from the throne of God in heaven those 36 inches would not mean all that much. So it is with our problems. We must learn to view them from God's perspective. If the difference between a giant and a dwarf is only 36 inches, the difference between great difficulties and small problems must measure about the same in the eyes of God. We must ask Him, as Caleb did, to enable us to see things from His perspective.

NEEDED: A CONSISTENT OBJECTIVE

The 10 spies not only lost their perspective, they also forgot their objective. They were not en route to Canaan to live in luxury and ease. They were going into Canaan to bless the world. They had been chosen by God from among the nations of the world and set apart to be the cradle of man's redemption. From Israel the Messiah would come.

Palestine, the land chosen to become Israel's home, was an isolated place. The Mediterranean Sea lay to the west; great deserts bounded the south and east; mountains were to the north. The Israelites were led by God into this land and were to live in virtual isolation from the idolatrous people who surrounded them. The nation was small and insignificant when measured on the scale of world importance. It would not achieve great ambitions of world conquest as did Rome, nor great intellectual achievements as did Greece, but its mission was to be far greater than either of them. It would be the training ground for a people who were to have a worldwide *spiritual* influence.

Although small and isolated, Israel was central among the leading nations of that time. It was about halfway between the western and eastern limits of the ancient world, and midway between the great continents of Asia and Africa. It belonged to neither but provided a communication link for both. The land, rich in natural resources, was capable of supplying the needs of the people. It was a land flowing with milk and honey. Where you have milk you have cows. Where you have honey you have bees, and where you have bees you have flowers.

So the land was an ideal choice by God for His people. They were to go in, rid the land of its wicked and idolatrous influences, and live as a separate people. If they went in and lived among the heathen—intermarrying with them, adopting their gods—they would be disqualified from bringing salvation to the world. They were a chosen people, going to a chosen land to accomplish the task God had chosen for them. But they lost sight of all that. Their objectives became clouded as they dwelt on the difficulties at hand.

So it is with us; we too easily fall into the same trap. What is our destiny, our mission, our reason for being? To live in ease and comfort? Has God chosen us that we might bask in the sunshine of His blessings and relax in our own good lives? Of course not. Our objective is to bless the entire world with the message of Jesus Christ. He has told us to go into all the world with the Gospel, to make disciples among all nations. Will it be easy? No, but neither is it optional.

Will we, like the Israelites, look at our tasks and turn our backs on the commission of Christ when we realize the hardships and difficulties involved? Or will we, like Caleb, rise to the occasion in the strength of the Lord and go forth?

NEEDED: CONFIDENCE IN THE LORD

The 10 spies also imagined the worst because of their own lack of confidence. "There we saw the giants, the sons of Anak, which come of the giants: and we were in our own sight as grasshoppers, and so we were in their sight" (Numbers 13:33, KJV). Because they were hopelessly outclassed in their own eyes, they thought that they must seem that way to their enemies as well. The facts, however, were quite different.

Rahab, one of the inhabitants of the land, said to two Israelites a generation later, "I know that the Lord has given you the land, and that the terror of you has fallen on us, and that all the inhabitants of the land have melted away before you. For we have heard how the Lord dried up the water of the Red Sea before you when you came out of Egypt, and what you did to the two kings of the Amorites who were beyond the Jordan, to Sihon and Og, whom you utterly destroyed. And when we heard it, our hearts melted and no courage remained in any man any longer because of you; for the Lord your God, He is God in heaven above and on earth beneath" (Joshua 2:9-11). God had dried up the Red Sea some 40 years before, and the Canaanites had been sitting there in terror of Israel ever since.

Imagine that! They knew they were licked. They had accepted that fact. They knew they were no match for the

God of the Hebrews. Fear had gripped them and melted their hearts. They were goners and knew it. Yet the people of God were as insects in their own eyes, and thought themselves no match for the giants they saw. Today, as then, everything depends on whether we look at life from ground level or from God's perspective.

The Apostle Paul challenges us at this point. The last letter he wrote was the Second Epistle to Timothy. The situation at the time he wrote the letter was bleak. In the East, the churches he had planted and nourished with his prayers and tears were being undermined by false teachers. In the West, a fierce persecution had arisen and Christians were being slaughtered by the most violent and inhuman means. Nero was herding them into the arena dressed in the skins of animals to be torn apart by wild dogs. Covered with pitch, they were fastened to poles and burned at night to provide light for the emperor's gardens and streets. Nero would ride in his chariot among them, drunk and naked, mocking them and revelling in their sufferings and deaths.

Meanwhile Paul himself was shivering in a cold Roman prison, awaiting execution for the "crime" of preaching the Gospel. His friends had forsaken him; he was alone. As he thought about it all, he wrote to Timothy and said in effect, "Isn't it great to be on the winning team?" (see 2 Timothy 2:7-13)

Paul's final declaration of faith and victory, his shout of triumph in the midst of seeming defeat, is one of the thrilling highlights of all his letters. "For I am already being poured out as a drink offering, and the time has come for my departure. I have fought the good fight, I have finished the race, I have kept the faith. Now there is in store for me the crown of righteousness, which the Lord, the righteous Judge, will award to me on that day—and not only to me, but also to all who have longed for His appearing" (2 Timothy 4:6-8).

There was no hint of doubt. He knew Christ would triumph. He himself would soon be in the presence of the Christ he had loved and served with all his heart and strength. The battle-scarred old veteran looked back over a long, hard, bitter struggle and announced the outcome: Jesus—victory! The devil—defeat! His perspective was true, his vision clear. Unlike the hesitant Hebrew spies, he saw things as they really were. No doubt he and Caleb have been having glorious, like-minded fellowship together in heaven these many years. God also has given us the grace to be among the band of noble and courageous souls who hear the heartening words of Christ, "Well done!"

NEEDED: FORGIVENESS

After the spies made their report, the people believed the worst. "Then all the congregation lifted up their voices and cried, and the people wept that night. And all the sons of Israel grumbled against Moses and Aaron; and the whole congregation said to them, 'Would that we had died in the land of Egypt! Or would that we had died in this wilderness! And why is the Lord bringing us into this land, to fall by the sword? Our wives and our little ones will become plunder; would it not be better for us to return to Egypt?' So they said to one another, 'Let us appoint a leader and return to Egypt' " (Numbers 14:1-4).

They rebelled against God and accused Him of murder, of bringing them all the way to Canaan just to kill them. In their folly, they prepared to elect new leadership and return to Egypt. How stupid! Would God guide them back across the burning desert by His pillars of cloud and fire? Would He feed them with manna?

Joshua and Caleb could stand it no longer. They said, "The land which we passed through to spy out is an exceedingly good land. If the Lord is pleased with us, then He will bring us into this land, and give it to us—a land which flows with milk and honey. Only do not rebel against the Lord; and do not fear the people of the land, for they shall be our prey. Their protection has been removed from them, and the Lord is with us; do not fear them" (Numbers 14:6-9).

But the people would not listen. Rather than face the unknown hardships of doing the will of God, they chose death. They wished to die because they were afraid of dying!

"But all the congregation said to stone them [Joshua, Caleb, Moses, and Aaron] with stones. Then the glory of the Lord appeared in the tent of meeting to all the sons of Israel" (Numbers 14:10). Notice something here. While the people shook their fists at God, blasphemed His name, and called Him a murderer, heaven was silent. But now when His men were in danger of being stoned to death, God was on the scene in a split second to protect them. He honored the courage of his faithful servants.

In an effort to save the people, Moses once again got on his knees before God, pleading His forgiveness, mercy, and patience on behalf of the people. "The Lord is slow to anger and abundant in lovingkindness, forgiving iniquity and transgression; but He will by no means clear the guilty; visiting the iniquity of the fathers on the children to the third and the fourth generations. Pardon, I pray, the iniquity of this people according to the greatness of Thy lovingkindness, just as Thou also hast forgiven this people, from Egypt even until now" (Numbers 14:18-19).

Once again the Lord heard Moses' prayer. "So the Lord said, 'I have pardoned them according to your word' " (Numbers 14:20).

The people had been too cowardly to enter the land. About the best they could do was prepare to stone Moses, Aaron, Caleb, and Joshua. That didn't take much courage, considering the odds were about 2,000,000 to 4 in their favor. Their problem was that they had forgotten the fifth Person with whom they had to deal—God Himself. "That is why I was angry with that generation, and I said, 'Their hearts are always going astray, and they have not known My ways.' So I declared an oath in My anger, 'They shall never enter My rest' " (Hebrews 3:10-11).

Caleb and Joshua, on the other hand, were allowed to enter Canaan. They had remembered God, relied on His promises, and displayed a God-given courage that had its moorings in faith. Today the eyes of the Lord are scanning the earth to discover such men and women of faith, and to show Himself strong in their behalf. May God grant us the courage to be the Joshuas and Calebs of our time.

TOPICS FOR STUDY

1. The source of courage in the lives of Noah and Abraham (see Genesis 6—9; 12—15).
2. The courage of David and his "mighty men" (1 Samuel 20—27; 2 Samuel 23).
3. How to face difficult decisions (see the Books of Ezra, Nehemiah, and Esther).
4. The exhortations to courage in the Book of Psalms.
5. The courage of the Early Church in the Book of Acts.
6. The courage of the Apostle Paul.

APPLICATION: What lessons about courage have I learned from this chapter? What must I do to begin making them a reality in my own life?

CHAPTER SEVEN

THE ENEMY OF THE BEST
The Lesson in Priorities

Study Material: Deuteronomy 1—8; 17—20; 30; 1 Kings 11—12; Psalms 20; 33; 48; Isaiah 6—8; Mark 12:28-33; Luke 9:18-27, 46-62; 14:15-35; Colossians 3:1-3; 1 Peter 5:2-6; 1 John 2:15-16

THE punishment had been severe. But then, the offense had been extremely grave. Not only had the Israelites displayed gross cowardice in the spy incident (see Chapter 6), but they had mocked the ability of God to take them successfully into the land. So the whole rebellious generation had perished in the wilderness. Only those who at the time of the incident had been 20 years old or younger —plus Moses, Caleb, and Joshua—had survived.

The final preparatory lesson the people of God needed to learn was the lesson of priorities. What is the focal point of life? Who is number one? What is involved in placing and keeping first things first?

In order for the new generation to possess the Promised Land, they had to keep their priorities straight. So Moses confirmed the covenant—which showed God to be their Redeemer and Lord—on the plains of Moab. On the threshold of the land of Canaan, he reviewed the lessons of the last 40 years and instructed the people in the priorities of life.

The Book of Deuteronomy does not needlessly repeat the Ten Commandments and other Hebrew laws. God confirmed His covenant to the new generation, and the laws that are repeated were given on the basis of 40 years' experience; many new principles were added as well.

The books of Exodus, Leviticus, and Numbers record the giving of laws from time to time, under various circumstances, along the people's journey. Now, with the trek across the desert ended, these laws needed reiteration. The Israelites, who had been pilgrims for 40 years, soon would be tilling crops and tending flocks in Canaan. The time had come for God to show them the applications of His laws to their new life-style.

Israel was about to enter a land polluted by the most hideous and obscene forms of idolatry. The tremendous need at this strategic hour was to drive home the basic principles of the Law of God. Most of the people who had seen the smoke, fire, and rumblings in the sky at Sinai when God gave the Law were no longer alive. With the exception of God's three-man team, the older generation had died, and only a small percentage of the younger people had any recollection of those awesome and memorable days when the Law was given. To the rest—those who had been born and raised in the desert—Sinai meant little or nothing. So it became a matter of urgency that Moses tell how the Law came into being and specify its place in their daily lives.

It was time as well for another rather unpleasant kind of review. The Israelites had to know of the tragedies and headaches that occurred as a result of their fathers' rebellious murmurings and lack of faith. Such background would help them learn how prone people are to wander, stumble, and fall. Hopefully they would also realize that the events that led to sin should actually have brought their parents into sweeter fellowship with the God who had never failed them. They needed to be reminded that their 40 years in the desert had been the result of lack of faith. Against the dark background of Israel's many sins, the faithfulness of God could now shine all the brighter. Time and again His power and goodness would be brought to their aid when all they really deserved was His wrath.

As they looked to the days of battle ahead, Moses once again focused their attention on the only One who could help. "The eternal God is a dwelling place, and underneath are the everlasting arms; and He drove out the enemy from before you, and said, 'Destroy!'" (Deuteronomy 33:27) God could be trusted. Their primary need was to discover what He wanted them to do and then do it. His commands and promises had to take priority in their lives.

PRIORITIES FOR KINGS

Moses gave the future leaders of Israel special instructions. Negatively and positively stated, these were to be the priorities for those who would lead in the everyday affairs of life. The instructions also were a prophecy of the institution of kings of Israel, according to the timetable of God.

"When you enter the land which the Lord your God gives you, and you possess it and live in it, and you say, 'I will set a king over me like all the nations who are around me,' you shall surely set a king over you whom the Lord your God chooses, one from among your countrymen you shall set as king over yourselves; you may not put a foreigner over yourselves who is not your countryman. Moreover, he shall not multiply horses for himself, nor shall he cause the people to return to Egypt to multiply horses, since the Lord has said to you, 'You shall never again return that way.' Neither shall he multiply wives for himself, lest his heart turn away; nor shall he greatly increase silver and gold for himself" (Deuteronomy 17:14-17).

The future kings were not to multiply horses, wives, or personal riches. These three things basically have to do with honor, pleasure, and wealth—misuse of which have snared men in high places down through the ages, and continues to do so today. They are, incidentally, the same three aspects of the world the Apostle John warns against (see 1 John 2:15-16): the lust of the flesh (multiplying wives), the lust of the eyes (multiplying riches), and the pride of life (multiplying horses).

First, the king was not to multiply horses—to take honor for himself. In a time when the common riding animal was a donkey or a mule, being seated on an elegant, high-stepping horse could lead to the snare of pride. Having a stable of horses would be like owning a fleet of Cadillacs today. I heard of a man in Las Vegas, Nevada who owns 30 Rolls Royces; one is even upholstered with ermine. These horses would be a similar status symbol to the king.

Furthermore, the king might begin to depend on his stable of horses. Later the psalmist would write, "Some boast in chariots, and some in horses; but we will boast in the name of the Lord, our God" (Psalm 20:7). And again, "A horse is a false hope for victory; nor does it deliver anyone by its great strength" (Psalm 33:17).

Second, the king was not to multiply wives—to feed the lust of the flesh. Carnal pleasure would eventually turn his heart from God.

Several centuries after Moses issued this warning, King Solomon tragically proved its validity. "King Solomon loved many foreign women along with the daughter of Pharaoh: Moabite, Ammonite, Edomite, Sidonian, and

Hittite women, from the nations concerning which the
Lord had said to the sons of Israel, 'You shall not associate with them, neither shall they associate with you,
for they will surely turn your heart away after their gods.'
Solomon held fast to these in love. And he had seven
hundred wives, princesses, and three hundred con-
cubines, and his wives turned his heart away" (1 Kings
11:1-3).

Third, the king was not to multiply riches. Why? Because he might become high-minded and proud, and lust
for even more riches. Then he might begin to oppress the
people through heavy taxation. That, too, happened during Solomon's reign.

After Solomon died and his son Rehoboam began to
reign, the people came and asked for relief: "Your father
made our yoke hard; therefore lighten the hard service of
your father and his heavy yoke which he put on us, and we
will serve you" (1 Kings 12:4). Rehoboam received the
wrong counsel from his buddies, ignored the advice of the
elders, and answered harshly that he was going to make
his father's taxation seem mild by comparison (1 Kings
12:10-14). So the kingdom divided, because a father and
son wanted to multiply riches.

In order to make certain that future kings would be
perpetually aware of these three danger signals, Moses
established that the king was to write his personal copy of
the Law. "And it shall be with him, and he shall read it all
the days of his life, that he may learn to fear the Lord his
God, by carefully observing all the words of this law and
these statutes, that his heart may not be lifted up above his
countrymen and that he may not turn aside from the
commandment, to the right or the left; in order that he and
his sons may continue long in his kingdom in the midst of
Israel" (Deuteronomy 17:19-20).

Note that the king was to do three positive things as well as avoiding the negative. One of the requirements God had of His king was to "write for himself a copy of this law" (17:18). He was to be a man of the Word; he was not merely to read the Word of God. He was to study it diligently, for copying would require long hours. And he was to continue this study all the days of his life. He was to be a faithful man of the Word.

Second, the king was to be a humble man. He was to learn to fear the Lord, to reverence Him properly, and to watch that his heart did not become lifted up above his countrymen (17:20). Centuries later, Peter writes that this requirement is necessary for today's leaders as well (1 Peter 5:2-6).

Third, the king was to be obedient to the Lord. He was to set an example that would be a blessing to all of Israel.

PRIORITIES FOR SERVING GOD

The religious leaders of Israel, the Levites, were neither to get entangled with everyday affairs nor concern themselves with material wealth. Their minds were to be free to concentrate on the things of the Lord. They would not share in the spoils of war nor in the land that would be divided among the people. Only spiritual work and spiritual warfare were to occupy their time (see Deuteronomy 18:1-2).

The other Israelites were to provide their food and fleece for their clothing (see 18:3-5). With that they should be content (see 1 Timothy 6:8). The priorities of God's appointed leaders were to be the things of the spirit. To enable them to serve the Lord without distraction, care was taken to provide for their daily needs.

I'm often asked by college-age men and women involved in the Navigator ministry throughout the United
States whether there is any difference between them and
their counterparts a generation ago, when I first became
involved in ministry for the Lord. They wonder how they
stack up with the Navigator teams of the "old days."

The training programs of today, I respond, are produc-
ing many more skillful Christian workers, not only among
The Navigators but throughout the churches. Today there
are many fine training opportunities available for Christians. Campus Crusade for Christ has large training programs in many cities. The "Evangelism Explosion"
ministry of the Coral Ridge Presbyterian Church has provided training for thousands of Christians in churches
across the land. Young men in the Southern Baptist
Church are actively discipling thousands of people. The
Bill Gothard seminars have been used of God to provide
training for thousands more.

Consequently people in almost every evangelical
church in America have received enough training to be
ready and able to lead an inquiring person to Christ.

But there is another side of the coin. I do not see the
same hunger for holiness of life that I observed in Christians a generation ago. Today I see a much more lax attitude toward the things of this world. Christians view films
and read books and magazines that Christians I met in the
"old days" wouldn't touch with a ten-foot pole.

Today's Christians may be better trained, but it concerns me that the intensity of spirit that seeks for a deeper
life in God Himself is missing. There doesn't seem to be
the same hatred for sin. Because it is easy for His people
to lower their standards and let down the bars against sin,
the Lord kept going back to the matter of purity of life in
His training program in the wilderness.

PRIORITIES IN WARFARE

In Scripture, God gave us His principles of war so that we might be prepared for spiritual victory. "When you go out to battle against your enemies and see horses and chariots and people more numerous than you, do not be afraid of them; for the Lord your God, who brought you up from the land of Egypt, is with you" (Deuteronomy 20:1).

The first rule for victory is *take the offensive*. The greatest defense is a good offense. "Resist the devil, and he will flee from you" (James 4:7). "The One who is in you is greater than the one who is in the world" (1 John 4:4).

One man and God is a majority in any crowd. Whatever your service in the cause of Christ may be, you can rest assured of the Lord's presence and guidance. Whatever your circumstances at the moment—cheery or heartbreaking, hard or easy, smooth sailing or rough going—you are called on to press ahead by faith. Are you bedridden? You can pray for the world and its needs. Are there conflicts or problems with finances in the family? Trust God to pull you through. Are you bewildered as to the will of God for your life? Rest in the confidence that the assurance of guidance is as basic in Scripture as is the assurance of salvation.

The second rule for victory is *not to be afraid* (see Deuteronomy 20:1). David, hounded by enemies who thirsted for his life, wrote, "When I am afraid, I will put my trust in Thee. In God, whose Word I praise, in God I have put my trust; I shall not be afraid. What can mere man do to me?" (Psalm 56:3-4) David did not let fear crush him and bring him to a standstill in his service for the Lord.

It is, of course, possible to be immobilized by fear.

During World War II, I watched a young Marine crack under heavy fire. In the center of unbelievable violence, gunfire, noise, and explosion, he suddenly stiffened and began to weep uncontrollably. Since we were under orders to move out, I had no recourse but to slap him smartly to get him moving. It was just what he needed. He regained his composure and carried on.

As Christians, we are never to be controlled by fear or anything else except the Holy Spirit of God. We're told to give every man who asks us a reason for our hope with meekness and fear (see 1 Peter 3:15). So if you feel a little meek and fearful about witnessing, praise God; you're on the right track. You qualify.

The third secret of victory is to *trust God.* Have faith. "Now it shall come about that when you are approaching the battle, the priest shall come near and speak to the people. And he shall say to them, 'Hear, O Israel, you are approaching the battle against your enemies today. Do not be fainthearted. Do not be afraid, or panic, or tremble before them, for the Lord your God is the One who goes with you, to fight for you against your enemies, to save you' " (Deuteronomy 20:2-4).

Following these exhortations, we come to an amazing passage of Scripture. Moses said, "Who is the man that has built a new house and has not dedicated it? Let him depart and return to his house, lest he die in the battle and another man dedicate it. And who is the man that has planted a vineyard and has not begun to use its fruit? Let him depart and return to his house, lest he die in the battle and another man begin to use its fruit. And who is the man that is engaged to a woman and has not married her? Let him depart and return to his house, lest he die in the battle and another man marry her" (20:5-7).

Though these commands were no doubt given for

humanitarian reasons, it is also true that the man who has his mind on things other than the battle will not make the best soldier. You can't rely on that man because his divided mind will not permit his heart to be fully in the battle.

This is an amazing passage because of its similarity to an incident in Jesus' ministry when He told a story about a certain man who had prepared a great supper and invited many to come to it. "But they all alike began to make excuses. The first said, 'I have just bought a field, and I must go and see it. Please excuse me.' Another said, 'I have just bought five yoke of oxen, and I'm on my way to try them out. Please excuse me.' Still another said, 'I just got married, so I can't come' " (Luke 14:18-20). Note the same three disqualifying interests: his possessions, his work, his wife. Whether we're talking about warfare or discipleship, the same principles hold true. If our minds are on worldly things—our possessions, our work, another person—our witness will be dimmed, our ministry hindered, and our fellowship broken.

This simple truth—taught by Moses in the Old Testament and Jesus in the New—has a practical application. Things perfectly lawful in themselves can become stumbling blocks if our affections become centered more on them than on God. A person's work, possessions, or wife can and should enhance his relationship with Christ. In the story Jesus told, however, the people involved clearly preferred things of time rather than of eternity. The man with the wife said, "I cannot." The truth is he would not. He could have gone and taken his wife with him.

The Apostle Paul's admonition along this line is always timely. "Since, then, you have been raised with Christ, set your hearts on things above, where Christ is seated at the right hand of God. Set your minds on things above, not on earthly things. For you died, and your life is now hidden with Christ in God" (Colossians 3:1-3).

Some time ago my son and I were watching an eclipse of the moon, observing the exact time when the earth moved between the sun and the moon. The moon, of course, has no light of its own but reflects the light of the sun. So when the earth comes in between, the moon is dark. As Christians, we are in a similar situation. Even though we are to "shine as lights in the world," we have no light of our own but merely reflect the light of Christ, the sun of our souls. So we must let nothing stand between us and God.

After dealing with the problem of other interests diverting the attention of some from the battle, Moses restated the need for faith rather than fear. "Then the officers shall speak further to the people, and they shall say, 'Who is the man that is afraid and fainthearted? Let him depart and return to his house, so that he might not make his brothers' hearts melt like his heart' " (Deuteronomy 20:8). An excellent picture of that principle in reverse is provided by the Prophet Isaiah, "You are not to fear what they fear or be in dread of it. It is the Lord of hosts whom you should regard as holy. And He shall be your fear" (Isaiah 8:12-13).

If somebody in your fellowship, for example, is always pointing out the dangers, problems, difficulties, and negative aspects of a given project, his fearful spirit will permeate the group.

PRIORITIES INVOLVE STRATEGY

Moses then instructed the Israelites on the necessity of strategy in battle. "When you besiege a city a long time, to make war against it in order to capture it, you shall not destroy its trees by swinging an axe against them; for you may eat from them, and you shall not cut them down. For is the tree of the field a man, that it should be besieged by you? Only the trees which you know are not fruit trees you shall destroy and cut down, that you may construct siegeworks against the city that is making war with you until it falls" (Deuteronomy 20:19-20).

I've seen people "cut down fruit trees" in their zeal to witness for Christ. A group of young Navigators, burdened to witness on a nearby military base, as civilians were not permitted to solicit on that base. Rather than use their heads, think their problem through, and pray about it, they ignored the regulations and like young bulls in a china closet went roaring in and began a button-holing operation. Soon the authorities booted them off the base.

Another group of young men, faced with an identical situation, took their burden to the Lord and sought His mind. One of them then decided to visit the base and share with the chaplain the burden of seeing men come to Christ. The chaplain, eager for some help, welcomed them with open arms. He made them part of his chapel team and gave them passes to get on the base. The men began to call on soldiers in the barracks on behalf of the chaplain and his program, and many men were won to Christ. The dwindling evening service suddenly took on new life as new converts came, gave their testimonies, and became involved in the program. Everyone was happy. The chaplain was delighted. The young men with the burden and the converts rejoiced, and so did the angels of God in heaven. In their eagerness to get the job done, the young men had not destroyed that which they would need for the long haul—the chaplain's goodwill and support.

THE FIRST PRIORITY RESTATED

Toward the end of the Book of Deuteronomy (chapter 30), Moses stresses several points. He continually uses the expression, "the Lord your God." What's Moses trying to say? He is reminding these people that they have a unique, personal relationship with God. This is something nobody else had. As a Christian, you also have a unique, personal relationship with God. He is the Lord your God.

Then Moses told his people to "*love* the Lord your God" (30:16, 20). He knew that a key essential of life was to love God with all their hearts and with all their souls. Many laws and commands had been given. Strategic lessons had been taught—lessons in faith, duty, worship, obedience, courage, and priorities. But now he brought them all together. What was behind them all? On what did they all rest? The key word was love.

Mark recorded a conversation between Jesus and a scribe, who asked, " 'Of all the commandments, which is the most important?'

" 'The most important one,' answered Jesus, 'is this: "Hear, O Israel, the Lord our God, the Lord is one; love the Lord your God with all your heart, with all your soul, with all your mind and with all your strength." The second is this: "Love your neighbor as yourself." There is no greater commandment than these.'

" 'Well said, teacher,' the man replied. 'You are right in saying that God is one and there is no other but Him. To love Him with all your heart, with all your understanding and with all your strength, and to love your neighbor as yourself is more important than all burnt offerings and sacrifices' " (Mark 12:28-33).

As the Israelites reflected on God's laws, His guidance through the desert, and His constant goodness, their hearts should have overflowed with love. If that had been the case, some of the problems and difficulties they had to face later as a nation would have been avoided.

Moses pulled it all together—for us as well as the Israelites—into the mighty theme of love. We show love for God as we obey Him. "Whoever has My commands and obeys them, he is the one who loves Me" (John 14:21). When we love God we will want to obey Him, to fulfill our responsibilities to Him in all areas of life.

THE ULTIMATE CHOICE

Moses told God's ancient people, "See, I have set before you today life and prosperity, and death and adversity" (Deuteronomy 30:15). Man is often motivated by the hope of good and the fear of evil. Moses continued, "I call heaven and earth to witness against you today, that I have set before you life and death, the blessing and the curse. So choose life in order that you may live, you and your descendants" (30:19). He told them that it was their decision, and that whatever they decided would affect them and the generations to follow. God was not casual about their choice; there was an urgency in His words spoken through Moses.

With that as a background, God sent Israel into the wars of Canaan. They were now ready to cross over the Jordan River into battle. And God was saying, "Remember your relationship to Me and love Me with all your heart and give Me your life this day."

Now what? What's next? These questions must have been on everyone's mind. In spite of all they had been through and the miracles they had seen—which ranged from the parting of the Red Sea to food falling from heaven—if they had known what was ahead it would have boggled their minds. Soon they would march around a great walled city and watch it tumble to the ground. To enable them to win another battle, the Lord would command the sun and moon to stand still. They were about to embark on one of the wildest and most exciting adventures ever experienced by any people in the history of the world.

One thing would become evident to them as they followed the Lord from victory to victory: there was no magic formula. God did not give them a set of buttons to push to ensure victory as they went from battle to battle. Great spiritual principles—such as faith and obedience—remained constant, but the battle tactics changed with each new encounter with the enemy.

Now, on the brink of battle, we're standing with Israel beside the turbulent rushing Jordan at flood stage. Fierce and awesome people are waiting on the other side. Let's see how God's training program in the wilderness prepared them for what was ahead.

TOPICS FOR STUDY

1. The problems with priorities that Jacob had (Genesis 25:27-34; 27—33).
2. The problems with priorities that Solomon had (the Book of Ecclesiastes).
3. Nehemiah's priorities (the Book of Nehemiah).
4. How the Prophet Haggai dealt with the priority issue (the Book of Haggai).
5. Jesus' teachings on priorities (the Gospels).
6. Paul's teachings on priorities (Paul's writings).

APPLICATION: What priorities should I establish in my life, based on the lessons of this chapter? Write them out.

PART TWO

D-DAY, CANAAN

Israel's Battles in the Land

CHAPTER EIGHT

GET SET . . .
Preparation for Battle

Study Material: Exodus 17; Numbers 13—14; Joshua 1—5

SPIRITUAL victory can be ours, but victory always presupposes a battle. There is no victory where there is no battle. And the victory-in-conflict theme runs through the grand sweep of the Bible. The first prophecy regarding the coming of Jesus Christ describes conflict and battle (see Genesis 3:15 and Chapter 1 of this book). The "bruisings" of the intense battle between the Messiah and the devil climaxed at the Cross of Calvary and will culminate in Satan's destruction in the lake of fire. From Genesis to Revelation, the Bible describes a conflict between right and wrong, good and evil, light and darkness.

God taught His people Israel great lessons as He brought them out of Egypt and took them into the Promised Land of Canaan. We have already considered some of the wilderness lessons of preparation. Now we will be looking at the battles in Canaan to discern principles for the Christian's spiritual victory.

Remember the words of the Apostle Paul: "These things happened to them as examples and were written down as warnings for us, on whom the fulfillment of the ages has come" (1 Corinthians 10:11). What happened to Israel in the Old Testament constitutes a lesson for *us*.

When we grasp that idea, it really brings the Old Testament to life. We see ourselves time and time again in the ancient account. We may see ourselves facing the walled city of Jericho, wondering how anything can happen without an assault. Or we may find ourselves standing next to David as he takes on Goliath—the giant who had kept the entire army of Israel at bay for days—and we can feel our stomach muscles tighten as we look up at his great height.

Battles, then, are necessary if victory is to be won. Canaan would be a place of battles . . . and victories.

INITIAL EXPOSURE TO BATTLE AND VICTORY

The people of Israel had just been redeemed from slavery in Egypt by the power of Almighty God—a picture of our redemption by Jesus Christ from the slavery of sin. They had also learned a lesson in faith (see Chapter 2) through God's miraculous provision of food and water in the wilderness.

Then, as soon as the Israelites had water to drink with their bread and quail and things were just great, Amalek came to fight against them. At that time, as in modern times, the enemy showed up unexpectedly when everything was going well. God allowed this to happen so His people would both learn the lesson of faith in practice and be prepared for the upcoming battles in the Promised Land.

"So Moses said to Joshua, 'Choose men for us, and go out, fight against Amalek. Tomorrow I will station myself on the top of the hill with the staff of God in my hand.' And Joshua did as Moses told him, and fought against Amalek; and Moses, Aaron, and Hur went up to the top of the hill.

So it came about when Moses held his hand up, that Israel prevailed, and when he let his hand down, Amalek prevailed" (Exodus 17:9-11).

This must have been an interesting sight to Moses, who knew that prayer was the secret to winning this battle. As his arms grew weary and dropped, the tide of battle turned against his troops in the valley below. "But Moses' hands were heavy. Then they took a stone and put it under him, and he sat on it; and Aaron and Hur supported his hands, one on one side and one on the other. Thus his hands were steady until the sun set. So Joshua overwhelmed Amalek and his people with the edge of the sword" (17:12-13). Note that during the battle Moses grew weary, but Joshua did not, a fact suggesting that the more spiritual the service, the greater the weariness that accompanies it.

This incident illustrates the fact that when we pray, the Lord will fight for us. The first battle was won by prayer. The Israelites remembered that victory by building a memorial to God; they knew that He had won the battle for them. They named the memorial Jehovah-nissi, which meant "The Lord is my Banner" (17:15). This theme is reflected in the New Testament cry, "Thanks be to God! He gives us the victory through our Lord Jesus Christ" (1 Corinthians 15:57). Christ is both our Joshua and our Moses typologically. He is our victory—the captain of our salvation (see Hebrews 2:10, KJV)—and our high priest who "always lives to intercede" for us (Hebrews 7:25).

Another lesson we can learn from this battle is that the enemy is a dirty fighter. Moses reminded the new generation of this on the plains of Moab. "Remember what Amalek did to you along the way when you came out from Egypt, how he met you along the way and attacked among you all the stragglers at your rear when you were faint and weary; and he did not fear God" (Deuteronomy 25:17-18). The devil is a dirty fighter; he is mean, ugly, and foul. Mark, in his gospel, called a demon "the foul spirit" (Mark 9:25, KJV).

In this preparatory battle, God taught the Israelites the nature of their enemy. Because in the days ahead they would face tremendous difficulties and launch into great wars, they needed to know early in their experiences how their enemies operated. Amalek, in this case, was not afraid to sneak up on them and pick off the aged, the weak, and the sick and murder them.

A third lesson that the people of God learned in this battle was that there was no magic formula for spiritual victory. At the Red Sea, the Egyptians approached them from behind and the Israelites were completely surrounded and in a hopeless position. God then directed the people to stand still and see their salvation. "The Lord will fight for you while you keep silent," Moses had told the people (Exodus 14:14).

Now they were attacked by Amalek and what were the orders? Stand still? No, God instructed them to choose men and go out to fight (17:9).

There is no magic formula. We cannot put God in a box. Victory comes only through Jesus Christ, but it comes in different ways.

PREPARATION OF THE LEADER—A SERVANT HEART

We have seen how God prepared the Israelites from the time they left Egypt till a new generation stood at the River Jordan ready to begin the conquest of Canaan (Chapters 2—7). The people who had been in abject slavery for centuries—their wills broken and their spirits crushed—were now, 40 years later, launching forth on a great venture for God. They were prepared because God had taught them; He had made them ready for conquest.

Now God spoke to Joshua, the new leader, and the first thing He said was, "Moses My servant is dead" (Joshua 1:2). All through Moses' ministry, he was known as "the servant of the Lord" and as "the man of God" (Deuteronomy 33:1). Here was a man who, having had the opportunity to be the king of Egypt, turned it down, saying in his heart, "I would rather be servant to God than king over Egypt" (see Hebrews 11:24-27).

What made Moses a man of God? The prime thing was his servant heart, a willingness to serve God and the people of God. His desire to serve God led to two traits that became foundational in his life: obedience and devotion. There is no fellowship with God apart from obedience. A person cannot commune with God if he is disobedient to Him. Also, there is no devotion to God apart from a willingness to obey Him. Both of these crucial traits grow out of a great desire to serve the Lord. Moses was the servant of the Lord.

We are also told that Joshua was Moses' servant (see Joshua 1:1). When God first chose a man to lead His people, He chose Moses, a man with a servant heart; when God chose a successor to that man, He chose another man with that same servant heart.

Why should God pay such careful attention to that one characteristic? Because a servant heart is the foundation for everything else in a leader. A man in a position of leadership who has never followed, who has never served another man, can be a tyrant. One of the worst men aboard a Navy ship is the boot ensign. Schooled to be an officer, he has not come up through the ranks. He comes on like gangbusters—barking orders, sticking his nose everywhere, demanding things. After a few years, he finally figures it all out, calms down, and becomes a good officer.

In light of the Bible's emphasis on servanthood, it is sad to see how much in-fighting and gouging has gone on in some Christian circles. In the Early Church, the only way one could get the job of overseer (or elder) was to convince everyone concerned that he did not want it.

Moses was a servant; Joshua was a servant. The best leader is the man who has the basic desire to serve. We also see this principle clearly exemplified in the New Testament. "Paul, a servant of Christ Jesus, called to be an apostle and set apart for the gospel of God" (Romans 1:1); "Paul, a servant of God and an apostle of Jesus Christ for the faith of God's elect and the knowledge of the truth that leads to godliness" (Titus 1:1). On these two occasions, when the Apostle Paul used the words *servant* and *apostle* in the same greeting, he put *servant* first. Why?

Paul did this because that's what he was—a servant. He was *called* to be an apostle—that was his job, his function. In his spirit and heart, however, he knew that he *was* a servant. And that is a great blessing, because there is always room for one more faithful servant.

We see this servant attitude also in the life of Stephen, one of seven men chosen to oversee the daily distribution of food to poor widows (see Acts 6:1-5). Now he could have responded to his selection something like this: "Are you out of your minds? Me serve tables for a bunch of cranky old Grecian women? You must be nuts! Don't you know to whom you are talking? Don't you know my qualifications? Why, I can quote practically the whole Old Testament. I've got a great grasp of the Word and a great ability to share the Gospel, and you want me to go over there and serve tables? Don't you think I am more fit for the limelight—at stage-center?''

Of course, that's not what he said at all. In fact, he was anxious to do whatever he could to help. We thank God that he was, because had he not gone into the pots and pans business, he would not have become stage-center for all eternity. That's exactly what he is, for there is only one first martyr of the Christian church. He would probably never have received that honor had he not first demonstrated a great servant heart by going out back and washing pots and pans and serving aged women.

Remember the Apostle Peter's word to the elders: ''Be shepherds of God's flock . . . eager to serve; not lording it over those entrusted to you, but being examples to the flock'' (1 Peter 5:2-3). Why not lord it over God's flock? Because the people already have a Lord—Jesus. The flock does not need another lord. If you look around the Christian enterprise, though, you'll find those who think that people do indeed need two lords—Jesus and themselves. That's not scriptural; God wants His leaders to be servants.

Jesus was quite precise about what He looked for in the leaders who would take over after He returned to heaven. ''You know that the rulers of the Gentiles lord it over them, and their high officials exercise authority over them. Not so with you. Instead, whoever wants to become great among you must be your servant, and whoever wants to be first must be your slave—just as the Son of Man did not come to be served, but to serve, and to give His life a ransom for many'' (Matthew 20:25-28). Jesus Himself gave us the supreme example of what it means to have a servant heart.

Over the years, people visiting Glen Eyrie, the international headquarters and conference grounds of The Navigators, have been amazed to learn, for example, that the fellow mowing the lawn has a Ph.D., or the one in the kitchen is a seminary graduate. These are men who have servant hearts. That's what God looks for in those who would lead for Him.*

GENERAL JOSHUA

After Moses' death, God chose Joshua to lead His people into the Promised Land.

Joshua's qualifications

God picked Joshua for three basic reasons: his courage, his faith, and his humility. Joshua was a man of courage, as his fighting against Amalek vividly demonstrated (Exodus 17:8-16). Actually, that is his first mention in the biblical record. Moses said, "Joshua, go get 'em!" And without hesitation Joshua went out to battle the Amalekites. We see his courage demonstrated again in the Kadesh-barnea incident when the report of the spies split 10-2. Joshua took the minority position then and also had the courage to stand beside Moses, Aaron, and Caleb against 2,000,000 people (see Numbers 13—14). Joshua was a man of courage.

Joshua was also a man of faith. God told him to lead the people into the land, so he said to his subordinates:

---

* More on this theme may be found in Chapter 4 of *Be the Leader You Were Meant to Be* by LeRoy Eims, published by Victor Books. This book may be obtained from your local Christian bookstore or from NavPress, P. O. Box 20, Colorado Springs, Colorado 80901.

"Pass through the midst of the camp and command the people, saying, 'Prepare provisions for yourselves, for within three days you are to cross this Jordan, to go in to possess the land which the Lord your God is giving you, to possess it' " (Joshua 1:11). He does not say "might" or "by the grace of God and with a little good luck it will all turn out OK," but stated simply, "We will go in and possess it!''

Basing his faith on the promises of God, Joshua took Him at His word. God had said, "Every place on which the sole of your foot treads, I have given it to you, just as I spoke to Moses" (Joshua 1:3). God had also said, "No man will be able to stand before you all the days of your life. Just as I have been with Moses, I will be with you; I will not fail you or forsake you" (1:5). Joshua believed these promises. Somewhere along the way, each of us needs to ask himself, *Have I been taking God at His word and moving out of my secure little rut by faith?*

Joshua was also a man of humility. Even with his abilities, he was willing to be Moses' servant. Through God's power, he learned how to live the attitude about which Peter later wrote: "Clothe yourselves with humility toward one another, because, 'God opposes the proud but gives grace to the humble.' Humble yourselves, therefore, under God's mighty hand, that He may lift you up in due time" (1 Peter 5:5-6).

While I was visiting with a missionary overseas, he looked me in the eye and said, "Well, LeRoy, I'm finally getting things straightened out, but it took a long time. When I came over here, I thought I was God's gift to missions. I was really going to change things because I had been so well-trained and equipped. My attitude not only spilled off on the people we were working with, but also on my fellow missionaries. They all knew I had come to get them squared away. Now that I look back on that past time, I can see that I did absolutely nothing. Zero!"

After a short pause, my missionary friend continued, "The Lord got through to me on that. I went before God and confessed the rottenness of my sin, and then I went to my fellow missionaries and confessed the whole business to them. And now God has begun to bless the ministry and things really look good."

Praise the Lord, it only took him a year to learn that principle. Did you know that it takes some people years and years to figure that out? And some never do. God does oppose our pride and can put up a formidable resistance to our self-willed attempts and attitudes. We cannot open a door He is holding closed.

Joshua's Communion With God

"After the death of Moses . . . The Lord spoke to Joshua" (Joshua 1:1). How did He do that? God had been speaking His Word to Moses before, but not to Joshua.

One of the key things Moses did before his death was to pray for a successor. "May the Lord, the God of the spirits of all flesh, appoint a man over the congregation, who will go out and come in before them, and who will lead them out and bring them in, that the congregation of the Lord may not be like sheep which have no shepherd" (Numbers 27:16-17). Here was Moses, on his knees before God, praying for a man to carry on. He had a concern for the people. Before God provided the man ordained to take Moses' place, he stirred Moses' heart to pray about it.

Success without a successor is failure. Moses, who knew that he did not have much time, did not occupy that time with regrets about himself. His primary concern was for the people. So the Lord answered him. "Take Joshua the son of Nun, a man in whom is the Spirit, and lay your hand on him; and have him stand before Eleazar the priest and before all the congregation; and commission him in their sight" (27:18-19).

Forty years earlier, after the tabernacle had been built, God had "called to Moses and spoke to him from the tent of meeting" (Leviticus 1:1). Now God said, "Behold, the time for you to die is near; call Joshua, and present yourselves at the tent of meeting, that I may commission him" (Deuteronomy 31:14).

Before Moses died, God commissioned Joshua. Moses had made certain that Joshua knew how to communicate with God through the tent of meeting and through the priest. Then, as now, a leader's first and foremost responsibility in helping people grow in Christ is to make sure that they know how to commune with God on a personal basis. As God reveals Himself to us through His Word, the Bible, we must make certain that others who look to us for leadership know how to study the Scriptures, listen to God's voice, apply His Word to their lives, and do not grow dependent on us.

Joshua's Firm Leadership

Joshua, the man of courage, faith, and humility, now took up the reins of leadership. When he came to the people, he did not say, "We hope to do this tomorrow," or, "We just might be able to cross this river." Instead he made a statement of faith: "Consecrate yourselves, for tomorrow the Lord will do wonders among you" (Joshua 3:5). God *will!* He continued, "Behold, the ark of the covenant of the Lord of all the earth is crossing over ahead of you into the Jordan" (3:11).

Put yourself in the place of these people. They face the

River Jordan at flood stage, knowing that the giant sons of Anak are waiting for them on the other side. It was a tense situation, and Joshua had to bolster their faith. "God, the Lord of all the earth, is with us," he said. "So let's go!" And they crossed the Jordan at flood stage.

Some have said this was not a good move by Joshua. Military tacticians have analyzed his orders and suggested that he made a wrong move. (As if God did not know what He was doing!) But God repeated the miracle of the crossing of the Red Sea, and the waters stood apart to let the people cross on dry ground. Tactically, it may have seemed a poor time to cross the Jordan, but two important factors need to be noted.

First, the Israelites crossed the Jordan at the time of harvest. The Bible tells us that "the Jordan overflows all its banks all the days of harvest" (Joshua 3:15). Joshua, in charge of feeding about 2,000,000 people, no doubt realized just how much food they would require. This was the ideal time to cross; everything in the fields of the land was ready to pick.

Second, if they had crossed the river at any other time, the landing would have been opposed. In both ancient and modern warfare, nothing is more difficult than landing on a beach in the face of determined opposition. But the enemies on the other side of the river were not expecting an invasion at this time. Knowing it would be a stupid attempt, they paid no attention to the activities on the eastern bank. Israel just walked over and sat down, totally unopposed.

Think also what effect this miracle would have had on the morale of the people living in Canaan as the word was passed. "They what? They walked across the Jordan River on dry ground while all the water was standing up? You've got to be kidding!"

"I'm serious. They're on our side of the river."

"You mean at flood stage? The waters did not stop them?"

That would be an impressive miracle for the Canaanites to hear about. They would begin to realize the power of God. Talk about a way to devastate the morale of the people and their will to resist! That was the way to do it. It was the perfect time to cross.

And it certainly had the right effect. "Now it came about when all the kings of the Amorites who were beyond the Jordan to the west, and all the kings of the Canaanites who were by the sea, heard how the Lord had dried up the waters of the Jordan before the sons of Israel until they had crossed, that their hearts melted, and there was no spirit in them any longer, because of the sons of Israel" (Joshua 5:1). The enemy fell apart. A military leader trained at West Point or Sandhurst may have done it differently, but Joshua did it God's way and succeeded.

Centuries later, Isaiah described the ways of God: "For My thoughts are not your thoughts, neither are your ways My ways, . . . for as the heavens are higher than the earth, so are My ways higher than your ways, and My thoughts than your thoughts" (Isaiah 55:8-9). Ask yourself how much higher the heavens are than the earth. The answer gives you an idea of the huge gap between the way we think and the way God thinks. It is always better to do things God's way.

ISRAEL IN CANAAN

The people of God, having crossed into Canaan while the Jordan was in flood stage, "burned their bridges behind them." They could not turn back. Now it was victory or death. God calls each of us to take that stand where there is no turning back, to make an unequivocal commitment.

A young man who came to the Lord at the Air Force Academy in Colorado Springs several years ago is back east teaching at The Citadel. After meeting Christ, he never looked back or glanced to either side, so far as I know. He made a straightforward commitment—dead ahead for Christ. It is such a blessing in this compromising and half-hearted age to see people, when they are converted to Christ, act like disciples.

The day of battle loomed on the horizon. For Israel, it was D-Day minus only hours. They had better have learned their lessons before this, for it was now too late for last-minute instruction. They were in enemy territory. Their lessons on faith, duty, worship, obedience, courage, and priorities would be all they needed for victory if they would remember to trust God.

The Israelites had also been taught that there was no magic formula for victory. They would have to learn that lesson again and again. So do we.

TOPICS FOR STUDY

1. The preparation of Joseph for his responsibilities (Genesis 37—50).
2. The preparation of David for kingship (1 Samuel 16—31; 2 Samuel 1:1—5:3).
3. The Bible's teaching on humility and servanthood (a topical study).
4. Leadership qualifications in the New Testament (a topical study).
5. Discipleship in the New Testament (a topical study).
6. The devotional life (quiet time).

APPLICATION: What principles have I learned in this chapter that I can start incorporating into my life? Write them out and how you are going to do it.

CHAPTER NINE

GO!
The Early Battles in the Land

Study Material: Joshua 1—8; 1 Timothy 6

IT was now D-Day, H-Hour. Joshua, who would lead the hosts of Israel in the battles for Canaan, met with God. The commander-in-chief of the armies of Israel was a man of courage, a man of faith, and a man of humility (see Chapter 8). He had been prepared for leadership by Moses, having served as his assistant for 40 years. Now responsible for the conquest of the Promised Land, Joshua needed further preparation.

THE PREPARATION OF JOSHUA

God revealed two basic things to Joshua before the conflicts in the land began. He gave Joshua a challenge to meditate on His Word, and confronted Him with His own Person.

The Challenge to Meditate

God, in His first appearance to Joshua after the death of Moses, said, "This book of the law shall not depart from your mouth, but you shall meditate on it day and night, so

that you may be careful to do according to all that is
written in it; for then you will make your way prosperous,
and then you will have success" (Joshua 1:8). Joshua was
to meditate on God's Word as part of his leadership responsibilities. This exercise would undergird him when
the going got tough during the campaigns in Canaan, and it
is meditation on God's Word that undergirds Christians of
any generation to face the situations of their day.

One problem many people have with meditation is that
they just cannot believe the great promises of God. His
promises seem so staggering that they often think, *It must
be some kind of oriental hyperbole, or it must apply to
another dispensation.* When God says something, He
means it. Paul stated, "No matter how many promises
God has made, they are 'Yes' in Christ. And so through
Him the 'Amen' is spoken by us to the glory of God"
(2 Corinthians 1:20).

The psalmist wrote of the tremendous benefits derived
from meditating on Scripture. "How blessed is the man
who does not walk in the counsel of the wicked, nor stand
in the path of sinners, nor sit in the seat of scoffers! But his
delight is in the law of the Lord, and in His law he medi-
tates day and night. And he will be like a tree firmly
planted by streams of water, which yields its fruit in its
season, and its leaf does not wither; and in whatever he
does, he prospers" (Psalm 1:1-3).

I've used this illustration in another book, but it is
pertinent here. Years ago when I was in London with Bud
Wiuff, a builder friend of mine from Iowa, we met a young
man named David Limebear. An active, agile, athletic
type of person, David was a typically loyal Englishman
who just loved his capital city. He was to be our guide for
the day.

He met us that morning with a timetable in one hand

and a map of London in the other. He had the city all
outlined. He knew where the undergrounds (subways)
went and what time they arrived and departed, and he
pointed out where we would go. Then we took off, full
speed ahead. It was quite an experience. We jogged
through the cathedrals, sprinted through the historic
buildings, and flashed by the great monuments. At the end
of the day, we were tired, but we had seen London. Or had
we?

A few years later, my wife, Virginia, and I went to
London. Our guide, a young man named James Fox, also
loved London, but he had a different personality. When
visiting a cathedral with him, we would sit down and pray.
When touring a historic site, we would take our time and
allow the fragrance of its history to permeate us. We took
the time to examine the monuments. I gained a completely
different perspective on that great city when I visited it
this second time.

God knew, when He commanded Joshua to meditate
on His Word, that no one can jog through Scripture and
get anything out of it. People who have been Christians for
a while must especially watch this unique danger. Since
we know the Bible so well (we think), we may just run
through it. This method will not work, though, because
God's promise is only given to those who will meditate on
His Word, to those who will revolve it in their minds. And
the reason we do it is that we might be obedient to the
Word of the Lord.

As I have thought about the definition and practice of
biblical meditation, I have found the following to be most
helpful. First I decide on a book of Scripture I want to
read. Then I get paper and a pen and go to the place where
I have covenanted to meet the Lord each morning. There I
get on my knees and pray, asking God to show me things

from His Word that will be helpful to me. "Open my eyes, that I may behold wonderful things from Thy law" (Psalm 119:18). After earnest prayer, I open my Bible to my selected section and read it through slowly.

As I read, I continue to pray that God will show me something that will be of great help in my own personal life. This can be in the form of a challenge, a promise, a blessing, a command, or a rebuke. When God speaks to my heart, I stop right there, and pray about what has been shown me. I ask Him to make it more clear to me, and to help me understand how it applies to my daily life practically.

After I have done that, I open my notebook and write down what it was that God showed me. Then I pray over that. I ask God to help me *do* whatever it is that I've written down, as a covenant with Him.

In summary, what I do is:

- I begin with prayer.
- I pray as I read that God will show me something that will be helpful to me in my daily experience as a Christian.
- When God does speak to me through His Word, I speak that back to Him in prayer.

So a complete circle is made. To me, this is real communion with God and meditation on His Word.*

Joshua was a man of great power and authority, but the first thing God told him was this: "Joshua, you are

---

* Another practical method of meditating on God's Word is given in *Meditation: The Bible Tells You How* by Jim Downing. This book is available through your local Christian bookstore or from NavPress, P.O. Box 20, Colorado Springs, Colorado 80901.

under the authority of this Book. You must live your life under the authority of the Word of God. That's the only way you can lead My people." That was Joshua's first order before he ever went into battle. And so it is with us— we too are under the authority of the Word of God.

Tied to the command to meditate on God's Word was a strong challenge and a comforting promise. "Have I not commanded you? Be strong and courageous! Do not tremble or be dismayed, for the Lord your God is with you wherever you go" (Joshua 1:9). Obviously, the source of Joshua's courage was the promised presence and guidance of God.

We read in the New Testament, "He (God) Himself has said, 'I will not in any way fail you *nor* give you up *nor* leave you without support. [I will] not, [I will] not, [I will] not in any degree leave you helpless, *nor* forsake *nor* let [you] down, [relax My hold on you].—Assuredly not!' " (Hebrews 13:5, AMP) This translation the best expression of the Greek quintuple negative, allows this verse to make as strong a statement as is possible in order to assure us that God will *NEVER* forsake one of His own.

The first time God gave me that verse, I jotted it down. A few weeks later, I met a man in Oklahoma whose farm had been totally destroyed by a flood. His assets were completely wiped out. I have never met a more dejected man in my life. He was sitting there amid the devastation with his head in his hands, really crushed.

I asked him if he believed the Bible, and he said, "You bet I do." So I gave him Hebrews 13:5. Imagine yourself, sitting there, having lost everything—your farm completely destroyed and all your crops gone—and you get this word from God. The man walked away that night clutching that verse.

When I met him a couple of years later, he said to me,

"LeRoy, all that year it was touch and go. We were hanging on by our fingernails. The one thing that I held to tighter than anything else was that one Bible verse. God so encouraged me with it that it saw me through the bad times."

The second source of Joshua's courage tied in to meditation was the certainty that he was in the center of God's will. He had been appointed to the task of leadership and knew that God was with him. When a Christian is in God's will and knows it, he has real courage to face life and its demands.

Third, Joshua had experienced God's faithfulness in the past. God had shown him the pillar of fire and the pillar of cloud. He had seen the manna and the other miracles of God. He knew that God's hand was on him and that God was in the midst of His people.

In an early psalm of David's, we read, "Remember His wonderful deeds which He has done, His marvels and the judgments from His mouth" (1 Chronicles 16:12). But here's a word of warning about the experiences of the past. They should only inspire us to faith. They do not give us a program or method for the future, because God may have something entirely different in mind. Remember, there is no magic formula.

The Confrontation with the Lord Himself

The second stage in God's preparation of Joshua for his leadership responsibilities was the appearance to him of a mysterious person, whom many Bible scholars believe to be the Lord Jesus Christ in a preincarnate form.

"Now it came about when Joshua was by Jericho, that he lifted up his eyes and looked, and behold, a Man was standing opposite him with His sword drawn in His hand,

and Joshua went to Him and said to Him, 'Are You for us or for our adversaries?' And He said, 'No, rather I indeed come now as captain of the host of the Lord.' And Joshua fell on his face to the earth, and bowed down, and said to Him, 'What has my Lord to say to His servant?' '' (Joshua 5:13-14)

A number of times in the Old Testament such manifestations of Christ occur. It is interesting to note that when He manifested Himself to Abraham the traveler, He appeared as a traveler (Genesis 18). When He appeared to Joshua the soldier, He did so as a soldier, with a sword in His hand.

Joshua responded correctly—he fell on his face, worshiped, and asked God for direction. "What has my Lord to say to His servant?" (Joshua 5:14) Paul, confronted by the Person of Jesus Christ centuries later, responded in a similar manner. "What shall I do, Lord?" he cried (Acts 22:10). Joshua and Paul each had the proper response when they saw Christ.

The foundation for victory must be laid on two precepts: a commitment to obedience to God through meditation on His Word and a sincere dedication of ourselves to the lordship of Christ as His servants. These applied to Joshua in his battles in Canaan and apply just as much to us in our spiritual warfare today.

THE FIRST BATTLE—JERICHO

Since Joshua was prepared and eager for the Lord's guidance, he listened to what God had to say about the strategy for the conquest of Jericho. He no doubt remembered that at the Red Sea the command had been to "stand still, and see the salvation of the Lord!" (Exodus 14:13,

KJV) Against Amalek, it had been: "Go out, fight!" (Exodus 17:9)

Now, at Jericho, God might have another approach; there was no magic formula.

"Now Jericho was tightly shut because of the sons of Israel; no one went out and no one came in. And the Lord said to Joshua, 'See, I have given Jericho into your hand, with its king and the valiant warriors. And you shall march around the city, all the men of war circling the city once. You shall do so for six days' " (Joshua 6:1-3).

There were to be no military preparations—no battering rams, no siege towers, no troop formations. The battle would be won strictly by faith, nothing else. God does not say here, "Stand still," or "Fight," but "March!"

Not only should we note what they were ordered to do—march—but we should note just how they did it. "And the armed men went before the priests who blew the trumpets, and the rear guard came after the ark, while they continued to blow the trumpets" (6:9). Armed men went first, followed by the priests, the ark, and the rest of the column. The ark was at the center of the army marching around the doomed city. What did the ark represent? The presence of God. This was the lesson to the Israelites: the Lord Himself was to be central in all they did.

We were having breakfast at our home one morning and one of the fellows living with us prayed, "Lord, be the center of all that we do today." That's the right idea. When that happens, we are on the victory team.

"So the people shouted, and priests blew the trumpets; and it came about, when the people heard the sound of the trumpet, that the people shouted with a great shout and the wall fell down flat, so that the people went up into the city, every man straight ahead, and they took the city" (6:20). Stand still? Fight? No, march and shout!

THE FIRST DEFEAT—AI

After the great victory at Jericho came a startling defeat at Ai. The account of that unhappy episode begins with the important little word *but*. That is an adversative conjunction, a word of contrast, and it really fits here. Things had been going extremely well; the Israelites had won a tremendous victory, but . . . . Earlier, God had placed a ban on the spoils of Jericho; they were to be consecrated to Him (see Joshua 6:18-19).

"But the sons of Israel acted unfaithfully in regard to the things under the ban, for Achan . . . took some of the things under the ban, therefore the anger of the Lord burned against the sons of Israel. Now Joshua sent men from Jericho to Ai, which is near Beth-aven, east of Bethel, and said to them, 'Go up and spy out the land.' So the men went up and spied out Ai" (7:1-2).

When my wife, Virginia, and I visited the Holy Land, we were traveling one day down a particular road. It was a cloudy day and the guide told us to look up ahead. There was a rift in the clouds, and the sun was beaming through on the ruins of a city on a hill. The guide asked us if we knew what city that was. We didn't, so he told us that it was Ai. I immediately began wondering how I would take that city militarily. What preparations would I make? How would I launch the attack?

"They [the spies] returned to Joshua and said to him, 'Do not let all the people go up; only about two or three thousand men need go up to Ai; do not make all the people toil up there, for they are few" (7:3). The spies made the decision for Joshua; no one consulted the Lord.

"So about three thousand men from the people went up there, but they fled from the men of Ai. And the men of Ai struck down about thirty-six of their men, and pursued them from the gate as far as Shebarim, and struck them down on the descent, so the hearts of the people melted and became as water'' (7:4-5). At Jericho they were victorious; at Ai they were defeated and chased. Why?

What did Joshua do when he got the news? Did he condemn the spies for poor intelligence? No, nor did he condemn the army for cowardice. He did the only thing he knew; he went to God. ''Joshua tore his clothes and fell to the earth on his face before the ark of the Lord until the evening, both he and the elders of Israel; and they put dust on their heads'' (7:6). There on his face before God, Joshua learned a lesson that also applies to us today: there is no way we can wage holy war with unholy lives.

God told Joshua, ''You cannot stand before your enemies until you have removed the things under the ban from your midst'' (7:13). Note that little word *cannot*. Here's the word for us on spiritual victory—we cannot expect victory from God while we are living in sin. It will not work. ''He who conceals his transgressions will not prosper, but he who confesses and forsakes them will find compassion'' (Proverbs 28:13).

After seeking God's face, Joshua learned why they had been defeated. There was sin in the camp. Achan, when he had been found out, confessed, ''Truly, I have sinned against the Lord, the God of Israel, and this is what I did; when I saw among the spoil a beautiful mantle from Shinar and two hundred shekels of silver and a bar of gold fifty shekels in weight, then I coveted them and took them; and behold, they are concealed in the earth inside my tent with the silver underneath it'' (7:20-21). The King James Version is really expressive here, ''I saw . . . a goodly Babylonish garment!'' Can't you just see that garment lying there? So Achan took all the spoils. They didn't do him too much good, for he had to bury them.

Notice the progression of sin here: I saw it . . . I coveted it . . . I took it . . . I concealed it. We see the same progression of sin in the Garden of Eden with Adam and Eve: they saw, they coveted, they took, and then they hid from God (Genesis 3).

Paul's testimony in this area is clear: "I have not coveted anyone's silver or gold or clothing" (Acts 20:33). If any of those people were wearing a "goodly Babylonish garment," Paul says that he had absolutely no desire for it. He sets forth a great claim in his letter to the church in Thessalonica: "You know we never used flattery, nor did we put on a mask to cover up greed—God is our witness. We were not looking for praise from men, not from you or anyone else" (1 Thessalonians 2:5-6). Paul repudiated worldly ambition and worldly gain. The empty wealth and praise of this world meant nothing to him.

Achan sinned despite God's plain warning. "As for you, only keep yourselves from the things under the ban, lest you covet them and take some of the things under the ban, so you would make the camp of Israel accursed and bring trouble on it. But all the silver and gold and articles of bronze and iron are holy to the Lord; they shall go into the treasury of the Lord" (Joshua 6:18-19). The Word of the Lord had been plain, and the people had understood it. Achan had violated God's command, and Israel's defeat at Ai was the result.

With God, nobody was a match for the people of Israel.

Without Him, they were no match for anyone.

Put a person in the Christian ministry into a prominent position and let him stand before people week after week. Pretty soon, if he's not careful, he will begin to think he's really something. He will listen proudly as people tell him what a great job he's doing. Then he may begin to use his position as a cloak of covetousness—as a means of getting wealth, power, and prestige. Remember, when Moses delegated his responsibilities, he was to share them with men of truth who hated covetousness (see Exodus 18:21, KJV). Why?

The answer is simple. Paul says, "Join with others in following my example, brothers, and take note of those who live according to the pattern we gave you. For, as I have often told you before and now say again even with tears, many live as enemies of the Cross of Christ. Their destiny is destruction, their god is their stomach, and their glory is in their shame. Their mind is on earthly things" (Philippians 3:17-19).

This is an interesting passage. These people were called the enemies of the Cross of Jesus Christ. Enemies not to the fact of the Cross, but to the spirit of the Cross. The spirit of the Cross is self-sacrificing love. A covetous person who is all wrapped up in earthly things is living exactly opposite to the spirit of self-sacrificing love. His mind is on the things of this world and on himself. Jesus said, "My kingdom is not of this world" (John 18:36). So we are given admonitions: "Do not love the world" (1 John 2:15), and, "Seek first His kingdom and His righteousness" (Matthew 6:33).

Achan's sin lay in the fact that he tried to use for himself that which rightly belonged to God. That's an easy mistake for us to fall into today. For example, our bodies are the temples of God; we have been bought with a price (see 1 Corinthians 6:19-20). Do we misuse them, devoting our energies to selfish pursuits instead of to God's service? (see Romans 6:13) The application of this principle gets right down to the practical level. It is obvious what God's outlook is when we see what happened to the whole camp of Israel because of one man's sin.

THE SECOND VICTORY—AI AGAIN

Having dealt with sin in the camp, Israel now could launch a new assault on Ai. This time they were going to do it God's way, after consultation with Him. They decided to march around it and blow trumpets as they did around Jericho, right? No, God had another plan.

God gave His instructions; Joshua repeated them. "See, you are going to ambush the city from behind it," Joshua directed. "Do not go very far from the city, but all of you be ready. Then I and all the people who are with me will approach the city. And it will come about when they come out to meet us as at the first, that we will flee before them. And they will come out after us until we have drawn them away from the city, for they will say, 'They are fleeing before us as at the first.' So we will flee before them. And you shall rise from your ambush and take possession of the city, for the Lord you God will deliver it into your hand. Then it will be when you have seized the city, that you shall set the city on fire. You shall do it according to the word of the Lord. See, I have commanded you" (Joshua 8:4-8).

God delivered the city into their hands, using a completely different tactic for winning the battle. Not standing still, not fighting while someone was praying, not marching around and shouting, but an ambush.

Then came another lesson. One of the basic principles of war in any textbook on military tactics and strategy is pursuit. Once you've got the enemy running, pursue him. But God's people did something completely different. They stopped and worshiped.

"Then Joshua built an altar to the Lord, the God of Israel, in Mount Ebal, just as Moses the servant of the Lord had commanded the sons of Israel [see

Deuteronomy 11:29-30; 27:2-5] . . . and they offered burnt offerings on it to the Lord, and sacrificed peace offerings. And he wrote there on the stones a copy of the Law of Moses, which he had written, in the presence of the sons of Israel . . . . Then afterward he read all the words of the law, the blessing and the curse, according to all that is written in the book of the law. There was not a word of all that Moses had commanded which Joshua did not read before all the assembly of Israel" (Joshua 8:30-35).

Can you believe that? After they got their army psyched up, mobilized, and moving, God said, "Stop the music! Everyone come to a Bible conference!"

"What?" the amazed Israelites must have asked.

"Yes, right now we're going to write the Law of Moses on some rocks."

"The whole Law?"

"Yes, everything; not one word will be left out."

Why? Because God knew what they needed at this point. Think about it. With all the spoils of Ai in their hands, they were now rich. All this treasure was theirs. What is likely to happen to people grown suddenly rich? Their hearts could be turned away from God.

God so wanted His people to succeed, to have a good and blessed life, that He went to unusual lengths to make sure they understood exactly what was involved. They were taught the Word of God and confronted with the blessings and curses of obedience and disobedience.

"People who want to get rich fall into temptation and a trap and into many foolish and harmful desires that plunge men into ruin and destruction. For the love of money is a root of all kinds of evil. Some people, eager for money, have wandered from the faith and pierced themselves with many griefs" (1 Timothy 6:9-10).

That had been Achan's problem. He probably had few possessions after those years of wandering in the wilderness, and he really wanted the loot of Jericho. If a poor person's consuming desire in life is to become rich, God warns through Paul that he will drown "in destruction and perdition" (see 6:9, KJV). It's bad enough to drown in clear water, but to drown in destruction and perdition is far worse.

Paul also wrote that those who are already rich have to be on guard too (see 1 Timothy 6:17-18). Of course, riches are not the real issue. It's the love of money, the coveting after more, and the putting of wealth first in life that the warning concerns.

As we have seen through the first battles in the land of Canaan, our strategy will always be changing, but our dependence on God for victory must remain total and constant. When Israel listened to God, victory was theirs. When they departed from the Lord's commandment, they met with shameful defeat. The same truth applies to our lives—we must depend on God and His Word.

TOPICS FOR STUDY

1. The teaching about meditation in Scripture (a topical study).
2. The teaching about lordship in Scripture—of Christ in the New Testament and of God in the Old (a topical study).
3. The importance of the devotional life.
4. Jericho in the Bible.
5. Compare the sin of Achan (Joshua 7) with the sin of Ananias and Sapphira (Acts 5).
6. The importance of dealing with sin in our lives before we can expect spiritual victory.

APPLICATION: What have I learned from the incidents of this chapter that can be applied to my life? How am I going to go about putting these principles into practice?

CHAPTER TEN

KEEP IT UP!
The Later Battles in the Land

Study Material: Joshua 9—22; 2 Samuel 22—23; 2 Kings 6;
1 Chronicles 20; Ephesians 6:10-20; 1 John 5:1-5

T HE Israelites had now established a firm beachhead in
Canaan. They had been victorious in the Promised
Land, but they had also suffered defeat. When they did
things God's way, they were victorious; when they disobeyed God, they were defeated. Slowly they learned the
valuable lesson that there was no magic formula for
victory—military or spiritual. And so it is today.

THE UNIFICATION OF THE ENEMY

"Now it came about when all the kings who were beyond
the Jordan, in the hill-country and in the lowland and on all
the coast of the Great Sea toward Lebanon, the Hittite and
the Amorite, the Canaanite, the Perizzite, the Hivite and
the Jebusite, heard of it, that they gathered themselves
together with one accord to fight with Joshua and with
Israel" (Joshua 9:1-2). The enemies united against the
people of God.

Whenever a friend of mine, who works in an office
building, goes out for a coffee break, his foulmouthed
pagan co-workers try to annoy him. They sit there and

make a project of it, uniting against him in their language and jokes. It is interesting how the people of the devil unite to get something done. As Jesus said, "If Satan is divided against himself, how can his kingdom stand?" (Luke 11:18) Satan definitely unites people against God. We find a vivid example of this evil unity in the New Testament, when two mortal enemies became friends in the process of their opposition to the Messiah of God. "That day Herod and Pilate became friends—before this they had been enemies" (Luke 23:12). In the common mistreatment of Jesus Christ, the Roman and the Idumean united. Our spiritual enemies follow this pattern as well.

On the other hand, sniping, divisions, complaining, and murmurings against one another are often found among Christians. What a sad picture, for the potential for unity among God's people is far greater than the world's potential. We can be bound together by the power of love, while the world's unity is based merely on mutual self-interest.

THE CRAFTINESS OF THE ENEMY—GIBEON

"When the inhabitants of Gibeon heard what Joshua had done to Jericho and to Ai, they also acted craftily and set out as envoys, and took worn-out sacks on their donkeys, and wineskins, worn-out and torn and mended" (Joshua 9:3-4). The devil and his minions are slick operators. For that reason he's called both a subtle serpent and a roaring lion; he is tricky and powerful. Scripture warns, "Trust in the Lord with all your heart, and do not lean on your own understanding. In all your ways acknowledge Him, and He will make your paths straight" (Proverbs 3:5-6). "Put on the full armor of God," the Bible also commands, "so

that you can take your stand against the devil's schemes"
(Ephesians 6:11).

The Gibeonites also had "worn-out and patched sandals on their feet, and worn-out clothes on themselves;
and all the bread of their provision was dry and had
become crumbled. And they went to Joshua to the camp at
Gilgal, and said to him and to the men of Israel, 'We have
come from a far country; now therefore, make a covenant
with us . . . . This our bread was warm when we took it for
our provisions out of our houses on the day that we left to
come to you; but now behold, it is dry and has become
crumbled. And these wineskins which we filled were new,
and behold, they are torn; and these our clothes and our
sandals are worn out because of the very long journey.' So
the men of Israel took some of their provisions, and did
not ask for the counsel of the Lord" (Joshua 9:5-6, 12-14).

We learn great lessons from this incident. Three basic
weapons are ours for spiritual victory. The first is the
Word of God. Jesus taught us to use the Word in our
battles with the devil. He said, "Man does not live on
bread alone, but on every word that comes from the
mouth of God" (Matthew 4:4). Jesus quoted Scripture
(see Deuteronomy 8:3) to defeat the enemy.

The second weapon is faith. "For everyone born of
God has overcome the world. This is the victory that has
overcome the world, even our faith. Who is it that over-
comes the world? Only he who believes that Jesus is the
Son of God" (1 John 5:4-5). The devil does everything in
his power to make sure that we don't get into the Word
consistently and that we don't really believe what God
says.

The third basic weapon for spiritual victory is dependence on God. We must not rely on our own logic, wisdom,
and understanding. We are not to rely on the flesh. "I

know, O Lord, that a man's way is not in himself; nor is it in a man who walks to direct his steps" (Jeremiah 10:23). This was Joshua's mistake here. He did not depend on God, but tried to direct his own steps.

These bedraggled characters showed up, and Joshua's advisors said, "Their stuff looks old, tastes old, feels old, and smells old, so they must be telling the truth." They judged on the basis of appearances. They leaned on their own understanding.

This situation was quite similar to the incident in the Garden of Eden (see Genesis 3). The devil in the guise of the serpent said, "Eat this and you'll be like God. Eat this, because it will be good for you; there will be great spiritual value in it. Your eyes will be opened and you'll know so much more. Think about it. This will affect your minds and you'll become very wise." That logic is parallel to someone standing on the street corner pushing dope: "Try this, it will be good for you."

We learned earlier in Chapter 8 that the devil is a dirty fighter, ugly and foul. Here we learn that he is a wily character, crafty and tricky. Our safeguard is to be in the Word, to walk by faith, and to depend constantly on God.

FAITH TO EXPECT THE UNUSUAL

Another lesson comes to us in the next battle campaign when the kings of southern Canaan formed a confederacy to fight against the people of God. "The five kings of the Amorites, the king of Jerusalem, the king of Hebron, the king of Jarmuth, the king of Lachish, and the king of Eglon, gathered together and went up, they with all their armies, and camped by Gibeon and fought against it" (Joshua 10:5).

But God encouraged His people: "Do not fear them, for I have given them into your hands; not one of them shall stand before you" (10:8). And God helped Israel win the battle by sending huge hailstones to rain down on the enemy. "There were more who died from the hailstones than those whom the sons of Israel killed with the sword" (10:11).

Then Joshua ran into a problem. It began to get dark before the battle was won. What would you do if God had promised you victory and then darkness came on the battlefield? You might say, "Well, we'll regroup and lay new plans tomorrow." Would it occur to you to ask the sun to stand still? Imagine that, and try to put yourself in Joshua's place.

So Joshua spoke with the Lord. He had a problem, and he went directly to God: "O sun, stand still at Gibeon, and O moon in the valley of Aijalon" (10:12). Imagine stepping forth before all your friends and saying that!

I read this statement, and asked myself, "LeRoy, when was the last time you asked God for a miracle?" Notice the result: "And there was no day like that before it or after it, when the Lord listened to the voice of a man; for the Lord fought for Israel" (10:14).

A similar situation occurred many centuries later. Elisha the prophet was out with the sons of the prophets, cutting wood. Then an accident happened: "But as one was felling a beam, the axe head fell into the water; and he cried out and said, 'Alas, my master! For it was borrowed' " (2 Kings 6:5). Did the man of God say, "OK, let's get the scuba gear and see if we can find it" and then go over to the careless man and say, "This is a great time to teach you a lesson on checking out the small details"?

No, Elisha responded differently. Had we been in charge of that project, we'd have used the incident as a great time to preach a sermon on the importance of little things. We'd have stressed the need to care for details, such as making sure that axe heads are securely attached to their handles. None of us would have thought of saying, "Let's have the thing swim to the top." But that is exactly what Elisha did, and, wonder of wonders, the axe head floated to the top of the water (6:6-7).

It seems that in our modern approach to the Christian life we have lost a great deal of immediate reliance on God. We try to figure everything out, examining every angle thoroughly. Of course, God expects us to use the resources He puts at our disposal. We aren't to look for miracle solutions to all our problems. But neither are we to leave God out of our thinking as if we had no other resources than men of this world have. Elisha did not think or act that way. Neither did Joshua. They knew God did the unusual in response to faith.

GOD'S METHOD IS PEOPLE

The word really got around. "Why, those people who just came out of the desert have cleaned up on the Canaanites in the central and southern parts of the land." The people in northern Canaan became quite concerned.

"Then it came about, when Jabin king of Hazor heard of it, that he sent to Jobab king of Madon and to the king of Shimron and to the king of Achshaph, and to the kings who were of the north in the hill country, and in the Arabah—south of Chinneroth and in the lowland and on the heights of Dor on the west—to the Canaanite on the east and on the west, and the Amorite and the Hittite and the Perizzite and the Jebusite in the hill country, and the Hivite at the foot of Hermon in the land of Mizpeh. And they came out, they and all their armies with them, as many people as the sand that is on the seashore, with very many horses and chariots. So all of these kings having agreed to meet, came and encamped together at the waters of Merom, to fight against Israel'' (Joshua 11:1-5).

The northerners united, and once more we see cooperation among the enemies of God. Again the Lord brought His people a message of encouragement: ''Do not be afraid because of them, for tomorrow at this time I will deliver all of them slain before Israel; you shall hamstring their horses and burn their chariots with fire'' (Joshua 11:6). Remember that one of Joshua's strongest points was courage, yet the Lord needed to encourage him from time to time. The emphasis again was on what the Lord was going to do through the army.

''And the Lord delivered them into the hand of Israel, so that they defeated them'' (11:8). Israel fought, but God wrought the victory. ''For by their own sword they did not possess the land; and their own arm did not save them; but Thy right hand, and Thine arm, and the light of Thy presence, for Thou didst favor them'' (Psalm 44:3). God gave them victory, but when we read the story, we realize that they were fighting from morning till night.

And that was the continuous pattern. There was constant battle. Yet it was not their swords that won their battles; it was God. When we get that principle figured out, it's a sign that we are growing and learning the lessons God intends. We must understand that God's method is to use people. Generally, when He wants to accomplish something on this earth, He uses us, and that's what He did at the Battle of the Waters of Merom.

This pattern repeats often in the Old Testament. ''Eleazar the son of Dodo the Ahohite . . . arose and struck the Philistines until his hand was weary and clung to the sword, and the Lord brought about a great victory that day" (2 Samuel 23:9-10). Have you ever worked with a hoe or hammer so long that you couldn't let go of it? This is what Eleazar did—he couldn't release his sword. After the battle was over, and Eleazar had gripped the sword so long that he couldn't open his hand, the writer says, "And the Lord brought about a great victory that day."

"Now after him was Shammah the son of Agee a Hararite. And the Philistines were gathered into a troop, where there was a plot of ground full of lentils, and the people fled from the Philistines. But he took his stand in the midst of the plot, defended it and struck the Philistines; and the Lord brought about a great victory" (23:11-12). God wrought a great victory, but not without Shammah; he was the instrument God used in this case.

Remember that fact in your church and in your community. We Christians are the instruments God uses to accomplish His purposes. It is God who will do the work, but He uses us (see Romans 15:18).

It's encouraging to note that Shammah and Eleazar, along with many other men, came to David when they were down and out. "Everyone who was in distress, and everyone who was in debt, and everyone who was discontented, gathered to him; and he became captain over them" (1 Samuel 22:2). These men had all sorts of problems, but in just a few years they became David's mighty men—stalwart, brave, courageous. God used them to bring about great victories, and He can also use you, however inadequate you may be right now.

To use one more example: "Now it came about after this, that war broke out at Gezer with the Philistines; then Sibbecai the Hushathite killed Sippai, one of the descendants of the giants, and they were subdued. And there was war with the Philistines again, and Elhanan the son of Jair killed Lahmi the brother of Goliath the Gittite, the shaft of whose spear was like a weaver's beam. And again there was war at Gath, where there was a man of great stature who had twenty-four fingers and toes, six fingers on each hand and six toes on each foot; and he also was descended from the giants. And when he taunted Israel, Jonathan the son of Shimea, David's brother, killed him. These were descended from the giants in Gath, and they fell by the hand of David and by the hand of his servants'' (1 Chronicles 20:4-8).

How many giant-killers were there in the army when Saul was king? None. Why? Because Saul himself was afraid of giants. *He* was not a giant-killer. Then David became king. Now how many giant-killers were there in the army? The place was crawling with them; Israel was knee-deep with giant-killers. Why? Because David, the giant-killer, was now leading the way.

The point here is that it takes one to make one. It took a giant-killer to produce giant-killers. That is why the Great Commission (recorded in five places in the New Testament) is always given to disciples. Why? Because it takes one to make one. It takes a disciple to produce disciples.

God never uses a lie to teach the truth. He will not use someone who is sloppy and down-at-the-heels in his prayer life to help another develop a strong prayer life. It takes one to make one. But God is the One who will bring about the victory.

THE LAST BATTLES ARE TOUGHEST

While the sons of Israel were at battle, conquering the Promised Land, there lurked a thought in their minds,

We've still got the children of Anak to face. Jericho, Ai, the kings of the south, the kings of the north—all had been conquered. But the children of Anak—the fiercest, biggest, toughest, wildest of the whole lot—remained. They were the giants of whom the 10 pessimistic spies had reported: "Nevertheless, the people who live in the land are strong, and the cities are fortified and very large; and moreover we saw the descendants of Anak there" (Numbers 13:28).

The last battles are always the toughest. As we progress through life, we begin to show signs of old age. Our bones begin to ache, and we begin to tire easily. Wheelchairs, loneliness, infirmity, a sense of uselessness, nursing homes, feeling unloved, loss of hearing, loss of sight, special diets, canes, and crutches await us. Those will be the last battles for many of us, and they will be extremely tough. We can look ahead and see those fearful enemies waiting.

But those who have learned to fight and to win the earlier victories of life will triumph in the last tough battles as well. What happened when Israel actually met the Anakim, whom their fathers had so feared? "Then Joshua came at that time and cut off the Anakim from the hill country, from Hebron, from Debir, from Anab and from all the hill country of Judah and from all the hill country of Israel. Joshua utterly destroyed them with their cities" (Joshua 11:21).

Joshua's personal life was one of strength and victory in old age as well. Toward the end of his life—after the land had been conquered and divided among the tribes of Israel—Joshua was still the same man of courage, faith, and dependence on God he had always been. In his farewell speech he said, "I am old, advanced in years. And you have seen all that the Lord your God has done to all these nations because of you, for the Lord your God is He who has been fighting for you" (Joshua 23:2-3).

Joshua looked back and traced the faithfulness of God. God had led the Israelites; He had fed them; He had fought for them. Joshua saw no reason to believe that God would forsake them in their last battles any more than in the first ones. God is faithful, and we can count on Him. He is in every battle with us.

TOPICS FOR STUDY

1. The military strategy of Joshua in his campaigns (the Book of Joshua).
2. The unity of the enemies of God versus the potential unity of Christians.
3. The weapons of our spiritual warfare: the Bible, faith, and dependence on God.
4. The importance of people in the plans of God (a topical study).
5. Discipleship and disciplemaking.
6. The armor of our spiritual warfare (Ephesians 6:10-20).

APPLICATION: What important lessons does this chapter teach me? How can I start applying these lessons to my own life?

CHAPTER ELEVEN

MIRACLES ABOUNDING
Battles in the Period of the Judges

Study Material: Judges 1—8.

THE Book of Judges is a rich source of further random but very important truths relating to Christian victory. One passage typifies the entire book: "Now the sons of Israel again did evil in the sight of the Lord. So the Lord strengthened Eglon the king of Moab against Israel, because they had done evil in the sight of the Lord" (Judges 3:12). This general pattern shows up repeatedly in the Book of Judges. Israel would degenerate spiritually and be oppressed by neighboring peoples as a punishment. The Israelites would then cry to God in repentance and He would raise up a judge or leader to restore them. A time of rest would follow and then the whole cycle would begin again.

Under the leadership of Othniel, Israel enjoyed a long period of peace. "Then the land had rest forty years. And Othniel the son of Kenaz died" (Judges 3:11). While Othniel lived, there were 40 good years, and then things fell apart. Why? There are three reasons. The first is the strange power of man's corrupt nature. We are prone to wander.

I like to read about gunfighters, sheriffs, and Indians of the Old West. Once I read a story about a stagecoach with a young schoolteacher and a drunken sot aboard going west. At one point in the journey the teacher began humming a hymn whose words reflected our proneness to wander. After a time of fidgeting, the drunk raised his hat, looked at her with bloodshot eyes, and said, "Woman, will you stop humming that!"

When she asked him why, he replied, "Brings back too many memories. Woman, I wrote that hymn." Here was a man who had wandered away from the biblical truths that he had written about in that hymn. The tendency to wander is truly in each of us, particularly when we neglect the Word of God.

Second, the people of Israel got into trouble because of the detrimental effects of their soft lives. They had lived for 40 years under the protection of Othniel and they got soft. They became secure, indulgent, wanton, undisciplined, dependent, and pampered. A soft life looks good from a distance, but is extremely harmful to those caught up in it.

The third reason for Israel's quick decline after Othniel's death was the lack of good leadership. As long as Othniel was alive, life was good. But after his death, everything collapsed. When Jesus, centuries later, saw people fainting like sheep without a shepherd because they had no leadership (see Matthew 9:36), He was moved with compassion. He knew how much people needed good leadership.

DEBORAH AND BARAK

Deborah and Barak led Israel to victory over the forces of King Jabin, which were commanded by General Sisera (see Judges 4). Their song of victory, recorded in Judges 5, contains an interesting comment about the reaction of one of the 12 tribes while some of the others were rallying to the battle. "Among the divisions of Reuben there were great resolves of heart. 'Why did you sit among the sheepfolds, to hear the piping for the flocks?' Among the divisions of Reuben there were great searchings of heart" (Judges 5:15-16). When the people of God were engaged in a great war, the tribe of Reuben had great intentions and serious concern. However, they ended up sitting down in the middle of their sheepfolds. Why? The sheepfold was warmer, more comfortable, and safer than battle. Their action exemplified the fear of trouble, the love of ease, and the pursuit of one's own interests placed higher than the call of God.

The Prophet Ezekiel made a startling comment about Sodom, a city utterly destroyed by God. We usually think of Sodom's sin as being primarily that of immorality. But Ezekiel wrote, "Behold, this was the guilt of your sister Sodom: she and her daughters had arrogance, abundant food, and careless ease, but she did not help the poor and needy" (Ezekiel 16:49). Fat with pleasure, self-indulgence, greed, and sloth, Sodom refused to offer help to needy people.

Reuben was not the only guilty tribe. We also read, "Why did Dan stay in ships? Asher sat at the seashore and remained by its landings" (Judges 5:17). Dan and Asher had commercial business ventures which took precedence over going into battle with their fellow Israelites.

Another interesting group mentioned in the song of Deborah and Barak is the inhabitants of Meroz. It is the only time the Bible mentions the name *Meroz,* and it is cursed by God. " 'Curse Meroz,' said the Angel of the Lord, 'utterly curse its inhabitants; because they did not come to the help of the Lord, to the help of the Lord against the warriors' " (5:23). Meroz was near; he heard the sound of battle and knew the need, but he turned his back.

Scripture says, "Do not withhold good from those to whom it is due, when it is in your power to do it" (Proverbs 3:27). Apparently God does not look lightly on this sin of omission, of choosing not to help in the Lord's work or in the lives of needy people. God condemned Sodom and cursed Meroz for it. What had Meroz done? What was his abomination? What was his terrible sin? Meroz said by his inaction, "I have no concern for you, I have no interest in you, and I have no desire to help you."

People who work together really have to band together in heart mind, soul, and spirit. In the New Testament, the words *one accord* occur 13 times, 11 times in the Book of Acts. Interestingly, no form of the word *love (agape)* ever appears in Acts, though some 319 occurrences of the term are used in the rest of the New Testament. Why? Perhaps because these are not the meditations of the apostles but the *acts* of the apostles. Their love expressed itself in "one-accord" actions. And so should ours. As believers, we are members of one body and are interdependent. We need each other.

Jesus said, "If two of you on earth agree about anything you ask for, it will be done for you by My Father in heaven" (Matthew 18:19). That word *agree* is the Greek word *sumphonia* from which our word *symphony* comes. What is Jesus trying to tell us? You know what a symphony is. It's not every man playing his own tune. On the other hand, it's not every man playing the same note on the same instrument either. A symphony is every person playing his own instrument in harmony with the person next to him. It involves working together so that the total sound is right.

In the Book of Acts, the apostles were of one accord, one mind, and singleness of heart. The Gospels also stress the idea of a symphony. The Apostle Paul sets forth the concept of a body (see 1 Corinthians 12, for example). All these show that Christians are supposed to work together. No one person has all the spiritual gifts; Jesus is the only One who had them all. The rest of us need each other to be complete. When God sees His people working together, He unleashes His great power in a way that does not happen when there are divisions, strife, and individualism.

We observed in the last chapter how the world often unites against Christ, putting divided Christians to shame. There is power in unity, even when it is a unity of the ungodly. "And the Lord said, 'Behold, they are one people, and they all have the same language. And this is what they began to do, and now nothing which they purpose to do will be impossible for them' " (Genesis 11:6). What was God observing? A holy and righteous cause? No, He was looking at people building the Tower of Babel. Even in an unrighteous, ungodly attempt, few things are impossible for people who are one in spirit.

If Christians would truly unite, we would see things in our midst that would absolutely amaze us. But it must begin with the right spirit and attitude in each of us. We must see the other person's interests as our own. When someone has a need and we can help, we must not sit in our sheepfolds like Reuben; we must not mind only our own business, like Dan and Asher; we must not turn our eyes away from the need, like Meroz.

"Curse Meroz . . . because they did not come to the help of the Lord" (Judges 5:23). Make no mistake. Failing to help the people of God is failing to help the Lord. And that's the way He sees it.

GIDEON

After Deborah and Barak defeated Jabin and the land had rest for 40 years, the Midianites began to oppress Israel. We read, "For they would come up with their livestock and their tents, they would come in like locusts for number . . . and they came into the land to devastate it" (Judges 6:5). The enemy came to devastate the land.

The Apostle Peter exhorts us, "Be self-controlled and alert. Your enemy the devil prowls around like a roaring lion looking for someone to devour" (1 Peter 5:8). That is an important thing to remember about the enemy. He is not prowling around seeking someone to nip at. He is not out just to harass you. He is out to devastate your life, to destroy you.

Midian's oppression brought two calamities on God's people. First, they began to live in dens and caves (see Judges 6:2), virtual prisoners in their own country. Their situation, of course, was contrary to the true spirit of the godly life. "If the Son sets you free," Jesus said, "you will be free indeed" (John 8:36). Though such freedom is one of the basic birthrights of a Christian, he can become trapped by his own lusts and weaknesses if he does not remain in fellowship with God.

In such an unfortunate state, he would be unable to receive another birthright of the child of God, namely, provision for his every need. "My God will meet all your needs according to His glorious riches in Christ Jesus" (Philippians 4:19). So the second calamity that befell Israel was total poverty. "And Israel was greatly impoverished because of the Midianites" (Judges 6:6, KJV). Christians who are overcome by sin will come to poverty—of soul if not of physical resources—unless they repent and turn back to God.

To rescue His people from their unhappy predicament, God raised up Gideon, a prudent and hard-working man. When God appeared to him, he was out alone threshing wheat at the winepress, to hide it from the Midianites. He was working, even though his servants could have been delegated to do the job. He did not use the threshing floor, as one would expect. If you travel in Palestine, you will see these threshing floors. They are nothing more than outcroppings of flat rocks right out in the open country. Gideon could easily have been seen by the enemy. However, since it was not time for the grapes to be harvested, no one would expect him to be at the winepress. Gideon was clearly using his head.

Jesus Himself admired diligence in work and called men with those traits to discipleship. He didn't want idlers in His small, intimate group. He called men who were mending their nets and working, who knew how to work hard at their given tasks. The same principle is true for us today; God chooses people who know how to work.

In spite of these good traits, Gideon lacked faith. Everything God said, Gideon doubted. God said, "The Lord is with you, O valiant warrior" (6:12), to which Gideon replied, "If the Lord is with us, why then has all this happened to us? And where are all His miracles which our fathers told us about, saying, 'Did not the Lord bring us up from Egypt?' But now the Lord has abandoned us and given us into the hand of Midian" (6:13). The facts are, of course, that God had not forsaken them; they had forsaken God.

Next, God told Gideon, "Go in this your strength and deliver Israel from the hand of Midian. Have I not sent you?" (6:14) But Gideon objected. "O Lord," he argued, "How shall I deliver Israel? Behold, my family is the least in Manasseh, and I am the youngest in my father's house"

(6:15). Gideon did not believe that he was the right man for the job.

Gideon's reaction is one that easily comes to all of us. Often when we receive a command from God to go and do something, our immediate response is, "Lord, You must have the wrong man." Like Gideon, we then begin to recite the reasons why we're not right for the job.

But God told Gideon, "Surely I will be with you, and you shall defeat Midian as one man" (6:16). All of his excuses were totally irrelevant. The point is that *God was going to be with him.* When Jesus gave His disciples the Great Commission, He said, "Surely I will be with you always" (Matthew 28:20). We can count on God's enabling presence whenever we set out to do anything in obedience to His call.

Jeremiah had an experience similar to that of Gideon. God called him, saying, "I have appointed you a prophet to the nations" (Jeremiah 1:5). Jeremiah responded with objections, "Alas, Lord God! Behold, I do not know how to speak, because I am a youth" (1:6). What was God's reply? "Do not be afraid of them, for I am with you" (1:8).

This pattern recurs throughout Scripture. God calls someone to a task and, when he begins to make excuses, God replies in effect, "Look, the only thing you have to remember is that I am with you in this. Trust Me and My strength. I'll be there."

Still doubting God's presence with him, Gideon asked for a sign and God responded immediately. Gideon, forced to believe, then realized that he had seen the Angel of the Lord face to face. "Alas, O Lord God!" he exclaimed (Judges 6:22). But after more encouragement from God, Gideon was ready to obey.

God then gave Gideon several tasks to do before his main call of delivering Israel from Midian. "Pull down the altar of Baal'' (6:25), and, ''Build an altar to the Lord your God'' (6:26). The task involved two steps. The first was to get rid of the altars of Baal. Pagan altars cannot be transferred to the worship of God. The second step was to provide a means for the worship of God.

Gideon obeyed, though he did it surreptitiously. ''Gideon took ten men of his servants and did as the Lord had spoken to him; and it came about, because he was too afraid of his father's household and the men of the city to do it by day, he did it by night. When the men of the city arose early in the morning, behold, the altar of Baal was torn down'' (6:27-28). These idol worshipers shame us as Christians, for they rose early in the morning and went to their altar. Over and over, I find this to be one of the great excuses Christians give. They tell me, ''LeRoy, I don't have time to pray.'' Yet the worshipers of Baal went to their altar early in the morning.

If you travel in any Muslim country, you will hear the people called to prayer early in the morning. Yet Christians have all kinds of excuses. ''Boy, LeRoy, you don't know how hard it is for me to get out of bed.'' Perhaps we need someone shouting in our windows to get us up out of bed like the Muslims have. But since we don't have that system, it's up to each of us personally. It's a question of self-discipline, which in turn relates to being filled with the Holy Spirit. ''But the fruit of the Spirit is . . . self-control'' (Galatians 5:22-23).

Though Gideon had obeyed God in the preliminary task of destroying the alter of Baal and building an altar to the Lord, he still had a serious problem. ''Then Gideon said to God, 'If Thou wilt deliver Israel through me, as Thou hast spoken, behold, I will put a fleece of wool on the threshing floor. If there is dew on the fleece only, and it is dry on all the ground, then I will know that Thou wilt deliver Israel through me, as Thou hast spoken.' And it was so. When he arose early the next morning and squeezed the fleece, he drained the dew from the fleece, a bowl full of water. Then Gideon said to God, 'Do not let Thine anger burn against me that I may speak once more; please let me make a test once more with the fleece, let it now be dry only on the fleece, and let there be dew on all the ground.' And God did so that night; for it was dry only on the fleece, and dew was on all the ground'' (Judges 6:36-40).

God did everything possible to strengthen Gideon's weak faith, even to granting these unusual signs. Sometimes the problems we go through as Christians, if we look behind the scenes, are designed by God to strengthen our faith.

One summer, I flew to Madrid and spent the first few days getting my biological clock adjusted to the time in that part of the world. I awoke about 1 A.M. (this was what I was trying to overcome) and decided to have my devotions. I turned to Mark 9 and read about the demon-possessed boy who was suffering many torments. The father said to Jesus, " 'If Thou canst do anything, have compassion on us, and help us.' Jesus said unto him, 'If thou canst believe, all things are possible to him that believeth' " (9:22-23, KJV). Notice that the father said, "If," and Jesus said, "If." The father said, 'If Thou,'' and Jesus said, "If thou." The father said, "If Thou canst *do*," and Jesus said, "If thou canst *believe*." The father said, "If Thou canst do *anything*," and Jesus said, "If thou canst believe, *all things*." The problem is never with Jesus, because He *is* able to meet all our needs if we put our trust in Him.

Gideon's problem was not with God. His problem was a lack of faith, which God was willing to provide. Gideon was going to need a lot of faith for the coming battle because of the way God was going to direct it. God was going to make a point. His objective was not simply to give people back their farms; He wanted to save the people from their sins. In order to do that—to teach them to trust and obey Him—the means of winning a victory over the Midianites was very important.

"The Lord said to Gideon, 'The people who are with you are too many for Me to give Midian into their hands, lest Israel become boastful, saying, "My own power has delivered me." Now therefore come, proclaim in the hearing of the people, saying, "Whoever is afraid and trembling, let him return and depart from Mount Gilead." ' So 22,000 people returned, but 10,000 remained" (Judges 7:2-3).

Why were 22,000 of Gideon's soldiers afraid to fight? Because they lacked faith. Just as faith is the root of courage, lack of faith is the root of fear. The opposite of faith is not doubt, but fear.

With Gideon's army down to 10,000 men, God said, "The people are still too many" (7:4). The test God gave Gideon's men to reduce their number involved the simple matter of how they would drink water. God was looking for men who had their minds on the battle. When they reached the water, most of Gideon's men stuck their faces down in it and drank to the full. Three hundred of them, though, lapped water from their hands, kept their eyes open, and so were alert at the same time. Readers who are athletes will understand this. Have you ever tried to compete loaded with water? How much value are you in that condition? Remember this: every man was thirsty, but few had their minds on the impending battle. Most of them had their minds on their own comforts and satisfaction. God said, "Get rid of those and keep these 300."

Here's the point. There are three types of people. To one type, Christ is *nothing*. In the world, we are surrounded by people like that. There are also people to whom Christ means *something*. Our churches are full of people with that attitude toward Jesus. Then there are those to whom Jesus Christ is *everything*. God always uses that last small group to accomplish His purposes on this earth. That's the point of the story of Gideon.

After one more confirmation of Gideon's faith, the battle began. Victory was won with the noise of trumpets and the shining of lamps from broken pitchers rather than by conventional methods. Can you imagine that? Gideon and his men didn't copy previously successful tactics. They didn't march around the enemy stronghold. They didn't hold up their leader's hands to pray. They did not stand still to see the salvation of God, or set an ambush. They blew horns and shined lamps from broken pitchers. There was no magic formula; every one of their battles was different.

Judges 8:1 is one place in Scripture where you can jot this in the margin of your Bible: *Wouldn't you know it!* "Then the men of Ephraim said to him, 'What is this thing you have done to us, not calling us when you went to fight against Midian?' And they contended with him vigorously." *Wouldn't you know it!* No sooner was the victory won than the children of Israel were ready to fight among themselves. Gideon's brethren tried to pick a quarrel with him. "Why didn't you call us?" they muttered. "We could have had some of the glory too. Why did you want to keep it all for yourself?"

Gideon's response anticipated what Solomon would write later, "A gentle answer turns away wrath, but a harsh word stirs up anger" (Proverbs 15:1). Gideon said, "What have I done now in comparison with you? Is not the gleaning of the grapes of Ephraim better than the vintage of Abiezer? God has given the leaders of Midian, Oreb and Zeeb into your hands; and what was I able to do in comparison with you?'' (Judges 8:2-3) It's not easy for us to respond as Gideon did. When we have done our best to fulfill the will of God—given it all we had—and someone comes along and takes us to task, criticizing us unjustly, it is very tough to be scriptural and act like Jesus. It is much easier to fight back.

But Gideon gave a soft answer, and the result was gratifying. "Then their anger toward him subsided when he said that" (8:3).

Every Christian leader needs to learn from Gideon's example. "And the Lord's servant must not quarrel; instead, he must be kind to everyone, able to teach, not resentful. Those who oppose him he must gently instruct, in the hope that God will give them a change of heart" (2 Timothy 2:24-25).

Yes, some battles are better won with soft words than with hard weapons.

TOPICS FOR STUDY

1. The cycles in the Book of Judges—sin, punishment, crying for help (repentance), restoration, rest.
2. The characters of the judges that made them usable by God.
3. Involvement and noninvolvement (a topical study).
4. The concept of the body in the New Testament—why Christians need one another.
5. The place of faith in fighting spiritual battles (a topical study).
6. The concept of confrontation as opposed to the use of "soft words."

APPLICATION: What lessons did I learn from this chapter and the Book of Judges? Write out how I can start putting some of these lessons into effect in my life.

CHAPTER TWELVE

DON'T PAY ATTENTION TO THE ODDS

Battles in the Days of Samuel and the Monarchy

Study Material: 1 Samuel 4—7; 10—17; 2 Samuel 5; 2 Kings 18—19; 2 Chronicles 20

THE latter part of the period of the judges was a pivotal time in the history of Israel. God's nation was now moving from the regional rulership of various judges toward the centralized rule of a king. As we study this period, we must remember that there is some chronological overlap between the Book of Judges and the Book of 1 Samuel. The scene for Samuel's ministry is set when we read, "Now the sons of Israel again did evil in the sight of the Lord, so that the Lord gave them into the hands of the Philistines forty years" (Judges 13:1).

SAMUEL

Samuel was one of the greatest men of the Old Testament. The last of the judges, he was also a prophet, and the priest who anointed Israel's first two kings, Saul and David. He grew up during Israel's 40-year period of oppression by the Philistines.

After about 20 of those years, Israel tried to break the yoke of their cruel oppressors. "Now Israel went out to meet the Philistines in battle and camped beside Ebenezer while the Philistines camped in Aphek. And the Philistines drew up in battle array to meet Israel. When the battle spread, Israel was defeated before the Philistines who killed about four thousand men on the battlefield" (1 Samuel 4:1-2). Israel's self-effort was doomed to failure from the start; the Israelites had not yet learned the predictable outcome of trying to fight the battles of God in the energy of their flesh.

Did the Israelites learn a lesson from their defeat? Did they repent or call on God? No. Instead, they did something unbelievable. The Israelites tried to blame God for their defeat. "The elders of Israel said, 'Why has the Lord defeated us today before the Philistines?' " Then they came up with this beautiful scheme: "Let us take to ourselves from Shiloh the ark of the covenant of the Lord, that *it* may come among us and deliver us from the power of our enemies" (4:3). This amounted to an attempt by the Israelites to get the aid of God while they continued to live in sin.

Scripture says, "The foolishness of man subverts his way, and his heart rages against the Lord" (Proverbs 19:3). These people decided on a scheme whereby they would force God to act on their behalf. To understand the foolishness of that decision, we need to be aware of the commands of God concerning the ark and where it was to be placed. The ark was to remain at Shiloh and the people were to worship *there*. But they didn't want to obey God's instruction; they wanted to bring the ark to the battlefield. They thought having the ark at the scene of the battle would force God to act for them.

What was the result? "So the Philistines fought and Israel was defeated, and every man fled to his tent, and the slaughter was very great; for there fell of Israel thirty thousand foot soldiers" (1 Samuel 4:10). That broke the back of the army. The troops scattered into small, disorganized groups and the enemy captured the ark of God. Seven months later, after a series of strange events, the Philistines returned the ark to Israel (see 1 Samuel 5-6).

"And it came about from the day that the ark remained at Kiriath-jearim that the time was long, for it was twenty years; and all the house of Israel lamented after the Lord" (7:2). Remember that Israel was to be in bondage for 40 years and that, after 20 years, they had tried to deliver themselves by the arm of the flesh. Twenty more years had elapsed since then, and Israel's 40-year bondage was now nearly over.

How did the Israelites finally overcome their enemies? What did they do? "Then Samuel spoke to all the house of Israel, saying, 'If you return to the Lord with all your heart, remove the foreign gods and the Ashtaroth from among you and direct your hearts to the Lord and serve Him alone; and He will deliver you from the hand of the Philistines" (7:3). The solution was so simple, and yet so hard for Israel to apply. Samuel reminded them of four things: (1) they were to return to God with all their hearts; (2) give up their idols because God tolerates no rivals; (3) get their hearts right with God; and (4) serve the Lord. Then He would deliver them.

Samuel continued, "Gather all Israel to Mizpah, and I will pray to the Lord for you" (7:5). Israel had one man praying—Samuel was on his knees before God. "The prayer of a righteous man is powerful and effective" (James 5:16).

The people heeded Samuel's call to repentance. "They gathered to Mizpah, and drew water and poured it out before the Lord, and fasted on that day, and said there, 'We have sinned against the Lord' " (1 Samuel 7:6).

What was the result? "Now when the Philistines

heard that the sons of Israel had gathered to Mizpah, the lords of the Philistines went up against Israel. And when the sons of Israel heard it, they were afraid of the Philistines" (7:7). So to whom did they turn? To their generals? To their statesmen? To their own efforts? No. Thank God, they had learned their lesson. They turned to a man who could pray. "Then the sons of Israel said to Samuel, 'Do not cease to cry to the Lord our God for us, that He may save us from the hand of the Philistines' " (7:8). They turned to an intercessor.

When trouble strikes, we don't turn to someone who throws a grand party, tells a good joke, or puts on a big feed. We turn to a person who can pray. These people finally learned that lesson. "The weapons we fight with are not the weapons of the world. On the contrary, they have divine power to tear down strongholds" (2 Corinthians 10:4). "Moses and Aaron were among [God's] priests, and Samuel was among those who called on His name" (Psalm 99:6). How would you like to have your name recorded by God as one who prayed?

With the attitude now displayed by Israel, God had no trouble whatever in giving them victory over the Philistines (see 1 Samuel 7:10-11). "Then Samuel took a stone and set it between Mizpah and Shen, and named it Ebenezer, saying, 'Thus far the Lord has helped us' " (7:12). This is a tremendous point. Samuel acknowledged that *the Lord* had helped them, not a religious act or Samuel's own prayers. We must remember that the Word is not that which gives victory. Nor is prayer the winning element. God, always God, is the key; the Word and prayer are means He uses to accomplish certain things in our lives. Though God uses His Word to clean up our lives, He does the work. Through prayer, He changes our attitudes.

"So the Philistines were subdued and they did not come any more within the border of Israel. And the hand of the Lord was against the Philistines all the days of Samuel" (7:13). One man on his knees did more than all the army, all the self-efforts, or all the religious acts Israel could muster. That man was in touch with God.

SAUL

One of the saddest chapters in the history of Israel concerns its first king, Saul. The people wanted a king like the other nations, someone they could look up to and follow. Samuel warned against it, but they persisted, and so Saul was made king. "When he stood among the people, he was taller than any of the people from his shoulders upward. And Samuel said to all the people, 'Do you see him whom the Lord has chosen? Surely there is no one like him among all the people.' So all the people shouted and said, 'Long live the king!' " (1 Samuel 10:23-24)

Saul has had many things said against him, but the fact is that he started out doing a great job. No doubt he knew the tremendous task ahead and was aware of his own failings and weaknesses. In any case, Saul accepted the job with a humble spirit (see 10:21-22). He did not immediately move in, start giving directives, and throwing his weight around. In fact, at first he quietly went back to his farming. "Now behold, Saul was coming from the field behind the oxen; and he said, 'What is the matter with the people that they weep?' " (11:5)

Saul's first opportunity to step in and perform a service for Israel came unexpectedly. A situation had arisen in which some of the people were in serious trouble. Nahash the Ammonite had besieged Jabesh-gilead and would spare the people only on one condition. He stated, "I will gouge out the right eye of every one of you, thus I will make it a reproach on all Israel" (11:2). In those days when a man went into battle, he carried a shield in one hand and a sword in the other. When he held up the shield, it blocked the vision of the left eye so that he could see well only with the right eye. If a man lost his right eye, he was severely handicapped; he could no longer protect himself. So the men of Jabesh would be able to hoe corn, tend sheep, and be slaves, but from that time on they would be helpless to defend themselves in battle.

When Saul heard of the siege, he realized immediately that Jabesh was in terrible trouble. So he stepped out by faith and God used him to deliver this city. Then the people acclaimed him, and said, "Who is he that said, 'Shall Saul reign over us?' Bring the men, that we may put them to death" (11:12). Some citizens had opposed Saul as king, but now popular sentiment had changed. "He's done a great job," people said. "Bring all those guys who complained and we will put them to death." But Saul forbade it. "Not a man shall be put to death this day, for today the Lord has accomplished deliverance in Israel" (11:13). Saul not only gave God all the credit for the victory, but also dealt graciously with those who had opposed him, even though, according to the customs of that day, he could have destroyed them.

Then, as time passed, a sinister change began to come into Saul's life. Samuel had given him explicit instructions from God to "Go down before me to Gilgal; and behold, I will come down to you to offer burnt offerings and sacrifice peace offerings. You shall wait seven days until I come to you and show you what you should do" (10:8). Saul went down to Gilgal and waited for Samuel. But after his troops became nervous and his military situation began deteriorating rapidly, on the seventh day he decided he could wait no longer. He stepped into the priests's role, which was forbidden to him, and made the offerings himself (see 13:7-9).

Saul had hardly finished making his improper offerings when Samuel appeared. "Samuel said to Saul, 'You have acted foolishly; you have not kept the commandment of the Lord your God, which He commanded you, for now the Lord would have established your kingdom over Israel forever. But now your kingdom shall not endure. The Lord has sought out for Himself a man after His own heart, and the Lord has appointed him as ruler over His people, because you have not kept what the Lord commanded you" (13:13-14).

Even though Saul began his rule with commendable humility, before long he fell away. His sin in this passage began with self-sufficiency, fear, and unbelief. Then he fell into self-justification. When Samuel came, Saul actually blamed Samuel for his actions and said he went ahead "Because I saw that the people were scattering from me, and that you did not come within the appointed days" (13:11). Saul lost his kingdom because of two or three hours of impatience. Samuel did come on the day appointed.

One of the easiest times for us to stray from the will of God is during those times when we come up to what looks like a blank wall. How tempted we are likely to be to take matters into our own hands when we see no way out. Abraham, for example, had been promised a son. But as the years passed, it didn't look to him as if there would ever be a son through his wife, Sarah. So he took Hagar as his concubine, and consequently strife erupted between Isaac and Ishmael that continues to bear bitter fruit and suffering to the present day.

DAVID

The story of David and Goliath is a familiar one. "Now the Philistines gathered their armies for battle" (1 Samuel 17:1). This action was a constant refrain in this period; the Philistines were constantly fighting against Israel.

When it seems our struggles go on indefinitely, we find ourselves wishing that our troubles would end. As long as we are in this body, however, we will have to fight "the Philistines."

"The Philistines gathered their armies for battle . . . . Then a champion came out from the armies of the Philistines named Goliath, from Gath, whose height was six cubits and a span" (1 Samuel 17:1, 4). Goliath then insulted both God and Israel and asked for a man to fight him. "When Saul and all Israel heard these words of the Philistine, they were dismayed and greatly afraid" (17:11). Why was Saul so frightened? His response was quite different when Nahash the Ammonite besieged Jabesh and wanted to put out the right eyes of the fighting men. Saul had moved forward with courage then because the Spirit of God was on him. Now Saul was out of touch with God. He was living in the energy of the flesh. When one Philistine threw down a challenge, Saul was terrified. He was the same man, but with one major difference—he was now out of fellowship with God.

In my years as a Christian, I have watched men who went out under the power of God and served valiantly in the cause of Christ. Then something happened to them and their testimony began to wane. At last, anything that came along would make them turn and run. Such a thing is terrible to see.

As soon as David arrived at the battle scene, his oldest brother, Eliab, tried to pick a fight with him. "Why have you come down?'' he asked David. "And with whom have you left those few sheep in the wilderness? I know your insolence and the wickedness of your heart; for you have come down in order to see the battle" (17:28).

"You're just goofing off," Eliab implied. And he tried to put David down by a sneering reference to his humble task as keeper of a few sheep. David's answer was short and simple. " 'What have I done now? Was it not just a question?' Then he turned away from him" (17:29-30).

Here we learn an important principle: had David gotten into a fight with his brother, he never would have taken on Goliath. That is often the reason "Goliaths" continue to stand out there and challenge us today. We spend too much time in the church fighting among ourselves to be able to deal effectively with them. Like David, we need to turn away from unjust critics and go on about the business of fighting the real enemy. We will never win the right victories if we are always fighting the wrong war at the wrong time in the wrong place and with the wrong enemy.

Goliath appeared big, gaudy, loud, powerful, and awesome. But David knew that the battle was essentially a spiritual one and relied completely on God. He told Goliath, "You come to me with a sword, a spear, and a javelin, but I come to you in the name of the Lord of hosts, the God of the armies of Israel, whom you have taunted" (17:45). He said God would give him the victory so that "all this assembly may know that the Lord does not deliver by sword or by spear; for the battle is the Lord's and He will give you into our hands" (17:47). And God did.

Another episode from David's life impressed on us again that there is no magic formula for victory. Shortly after David became king over all Israel, the Philistines moved against him. "Then David inquired of the Lord, saying, 'Shall I go up against the Philistines? Wilt Thou give them into my hand?' And the Lord said to David, 'Go up, for I will certainly give the Philistines into your hand' " (2 Samuel 5:19).

You would think by now, with the Philistines having attacked so many times over the years, that David would have known what to do. Yet he asked God, and God gave him victory. But what happened next? "Now the Philistines came up once again" (5:22). "And when David inquired of the Lord, He said, 'You shall not go directly up' " (5:23).

What if David had said, "Of course we know what to do; we've been doing it for hundreds of years. Every time the Philistines come near, we go up"? Then David would have erred this time, for God had a different approach in mind. God is creative and resourceful. Instead of giving us one pat formula for victory, He wants us to come to Him regularly for new instructions and new strategy.

JEHOSHAPHAT

Another means by which God gave victory in battle came during the reign of King Jehoshaphat. "Now it came about after this that the sons of Moab and the sons of Ammon, together with some of the Meunites, came to make war against Jehoshaphat" (2 Chronicles 20:1). Let's try to look at this scene in perspective: it would be as though the entire Chinese army were to surround Rexford, Kansas. The odds here were that lopsided; the situation was utterly hopeless. There was no way out.

King Jehoshaphat and the people of Judah prayed earnestly. "O our God, wilt Thou not judge them? For we

are powerless before this great multitude who are coming
against us; nor do we know what to do, but our eyes are on
Thee" (20:12). Isn't that beautiful? They were saying,
"Lord, we haven't the faintest idea what to do. We don't
have any answers but we are looking to You." That was a
powerful request.

God's reply through His prophet was clear, "You
need not fight in this battle; station yourselves, stand and
see the salvation of the Lord on your behalf, O Judah and
Jerusalem" (20:17). This sounds like the instructions God
gave the Israelites centuries before when they were
threatened with annihilation at the Red Sea.

Jehoshaphat led his people forth, exhorting them to
"put your trust in the Lord your God, and you will be
established" (20:20). Then he did an unbelievable thing:
"When he had consulted with the people, he appointed
those who sang to the Lord and those who praised Him in
holy attire, as they went out before the army and said,
'Give thanks to the Lord, for His lovingkindness is everlasting' " (20:21).

During my service in the Marine Corps, I can't remember one time when our commander put a choir out in
front of the first wave of infantry. In fact, this was the first,
last, and only time in recorded history that such a thing
has ever occurred. I don't know where Jehoshaphat even
got the idea, but apparently he was so confident in God's
promise that he wanted to express his praise.

Through their praise, thanksgiving, and faith, the Israelites won a great victory. Their enemies fought among
themselves and all Israel had to do was to spend three
days taking home the spoils.

Thanksgiving must be part of a believer's life-style.
There will be times in each of our lives when things are so
desperate that we will lose even the strength to pray. That

will leave only one thing to do: praise the Lord. And as you praise Him in faith, He will give the victory.

HEZEKIAH

The last pattern for victory that we want to examine was given by God to His people during the reign of King Hezekiah. "Now in the fourteenth year of King Hezekiah, Sennacherib king of Assyria came up against all the fortified cities of Judah and seized them" (2 Kings 18:13). Hezekiah tried to appease his enemy, and "gave him all the silver which was found in the house of the Lord, and in the treasuries of the king's house. At that time Hezekiah cut off the gold from the doors of the temple of the Lord, and from the doorposts which Hezekiah king of Judah had overlaid, and gave it to the king of Assyria" (18:15-16).

Did his attempt to buy off Sennacherib work? No, for all Sennacherib did was mount another attack. "Then the king of Assyria sent . . . a large army to Jerusalem" (18:17). Buying him off didn't work. Similarly, we cannot make deals with the enemy. We cannot bargain with him. The only thing we can do is resist. "Resist the devil, and he will flee from you" (James 4:7).

The king of Assyria then launched a heavy propaganda campaign against Hezekiah. He told the people of God, "Do not listen to Hezekiah, for thus says the king of Assyria, 'Make your peace with me and come out to me, and eat each of his vine and each of his fig tree and drink each of the waters of his own cistern, until I come and take you away to a land like your own land, a land of grain and new wine, a land of bread and vineyards, a land of olive trees and honey, that you may live and not die.' But do not listen to Hezekiah, when he misleads you, saying, 'The Lord will deliver us.' Has any one of the gods of the nations delivered his land from the hand of the king of Assyria?'' (2 Kings 18:31-33)

Have you ever heard any promises like those? ''Surrender to me and I will make you prosperous and happy. You'll live in a fine situation. You will have a great life. All you have to do is come my way.'' That is still the devil's appeal today. The enemy never changes his tactics. He's been at his business a long time, and he knows how to lure people into his traps. He makes people think his way is great, while God's is hard, narrow, and austere.

Note Hezekiah's reaction. ''When King Hezekiah heard it, he tore his clothes, covered himself with sackcloth and entered the house of the Lord'' (2 Kings 19:1). Then he did a wise thing; he sent a messenger to Isaiah, the prophet, asking for prayer (see 19:2-4).

Isaiah assured Hezekiah that God would deal with the army of Sennacherib. ''Then it happened that night that the angel of the Lord went out, and struck 185,000 in the camp of the Assyrians; and when men rose early in the morning, behold, all of them were dead bodies'' (19:35). The battle was won through the prayer of one man, Isaiah.

What was Sennacherib's problem? He was a proud man. He thought, *Nobody can defy me*. Sometimes I meet people like that. They say they know the Bible and then they begin to ask tricky questions, as if they know more than God does. I've met them by the score and I wouldn't want to be in their places on a certain day. The Bible talks about men who speak great swelling words (see 2 Peter 2:18; Jude 16). One of these days those great swelling words will burst and the truth will be known. A time is coming when we are all going to stand before God, alone, with no way to hide.

God hates the sin of pride. David fell into this sin when "Satan stood up against Israel and moved David to number Israel" (1 Chronicles 21:1). This act, motivated by pride on David's part, was a needless venture. David simply wanted to gloat over the size of his kingdom. "God was displeased with this thing, so He struck Israel" (21:7).

How many men were lost as a result of this particular sin in the life of David? At least 70,000 died (see 2 Samuel 24:15). How many lives were lost as a result of David's immorality with Bathsheba? Two. In God's sight, sin is sin. However, the pestilence sent on Israel exemplifies the great hatred God has toward pride. He hates it because it is the prime tool of the devil to keep men and women from kneeling at the Cross of Jesus Christ. That sin, when it keeps men from kneeling at the Cross of Christ, seals their eternal destruction.

Throughout all of Israel's history, God worked in different ways in giving victory to His people. There was no magic formula, and only the men of faith prevailed. Those like Saul, who tried doing things their own way, failed. But Samuel, David, Jehoshaphat, and Hezekiah were men who trusted God and prevailed. Across the centuries, they call us to follow their examples.

TOPICS FOR STUDY

1. The life and ministry of Samuel (1 Samuel 1—12).
2. Contrast the personalities and activities of Saul and David (1 Samuel 9—2 Samuel 4).
3. The tragic results of self-will in the Bible (a topical study).
4. The awful sin of pride (a topical study).
5. The influence of the Prophet Isaiah on King Hezekiah.
6. The tactics of the devil (a topical study).

APPLICATION: What specific lessons did I learn from this segment of Israel's history? How am I going to apply these lessons to my life today?

CHAPTER THIRTEEN

NO MAGIC FORMULA

Study Material: Joshua 23—24

WHENEVER it is time to say "good-bye," I usually shed a few tears. I try to hide them, but they are there, regardless if the parting is for a few days, a month, or a year.

"Hellos," on the other hand, are great. It's fun to be on an arriving plane and watch a grandmother getting ready to greet the children, and then to see the meeting itself full of joy, hugs, and kisses. But for everyone involved, it's no fun at all to turn around and say good-bye. Hugs and kisses appear once more, but with tears this time.

The Bible records some good-byes: Paul on the shores of Miletus bidding farewell to the elders of the Ephesian church; David saying good-bye to Solomon; Jacob rising from his deathbed to say a few last words to his sons.

As we come to the end of our study on spiritual warfare and victory, we will consider one good-bye speech— the closing words of Joshua after the Lord had given rest to Israel from all her enemies.

This speech was a final charge from a leader who had been with his people from their days of slavery in Egypt to the final conquest of Canaan. Joshua had seen and experienced it all: the deliverance from Egypt, the parting of the Red Sea, the provision of the manna, the giving of the Ten Commandments, the curse of the fiery serpents in the wilderness, and much more. He had experienced all these things with the people. And he had led them to victory in Canaan.

Now, nearing death, Joshua called on the new generation to take both a forward and a backward look, as Moses had done before him. He reminded them of five important things.

THE FACT OF GOD'S INTEGRITY

" 'I am old, advanced in years,' [Joshua] said to the assembled crowd. 'And you have seen all that the Lord your God has done to all these nations because of you, for the Lord your God is He who has been fighting for you . . . . And the Lord your God, He shall thrust them out from before you and drive them from before you; and you shall possess their land, just as the Lord your God promised you' " (Joshua 23:2-3, 5).

The first was the fact of God's integrity. God had done all that He had promised in the past, and therefore could be relied on in the future. God is faithful.

We all need this reminder from time to time. Life has a way of pressing in on us. Unexpected things occur that throw our carefully made plans to the wind. Our orderly lives suddenly are caught in the tornadoes of trouble and hard times. Yet if we keep the inner eye of our spirits focused on the faithfulness of God, we can deal with our problems in proper perspective.

The temptations of Jesus throw light on this. In the first temptation, He was tempted to doubt God's faithfulness. "The tempter came to Him and said, 'If You are the Son of God, tell these stones to become bread' " (Matthew 4:3). Jesus could have done it, of course. If He could turn water into wine (see John 2:1-11), He certainly could turn stones into bread. But He didn't. He faced the temptation, overcame it, and left us an example of how to counter temptation with the Word of God.

What was the nature of the temptation? The devil said in effect, "God has left You out here to starve. He has forgotten all about You. You are alone and hungry. You'd better take the matter into Your own hands. If You are going to survive, it's up to You. You can't count on God for any help. He has abandoned You to the wilderness." Isn't it interesting that the devil did not challenge Jesus to pray about it, to have Him ask God to change the stones into bread?

This temptation is common to all men. *Does God know my situation?* we wonder. *Does God care? Does God love me?* Such thoughts and questions naturally arise when the bottom drops out of our plans and dreams. But Joshua, knowing Israel would still face some battles and difficulties, also understood the truth of Moses' words to the people a generation earlier. "The eternal God is thy refuge, and underneath are the everlasting arms" (Deuteronomy 33:27, KJV). So Joshua reminded the new generation of the faithfulness of God.

THE COURAGE TO LIVE ACCORDING TO GOD'S WORD

Joshua's second farewell statement exhorted the Israelites to have the courage to live according to the Word of God. "Be very firm, then, to keep and do all that is written in the book of the law of Moses, so that you may not turn aside from it to the right hand or to the left" (Joshua 23:6). He was passing on to his successors the same word he had received from God some 30 years earlier. At that time, the Lord had promised him prosperity and success, and concluded with, "Have I not commanded you? Be strong and courageous!" (Joshua 1:7-9)

Here again, we need to pay careful attention to this call or direction for our lives. We are not only to live *according* to God's Word, but to live within its limits. We are under its authority. Joshua had been told to meditate on the Word that he might learn "to do according to all that is written in it" (1:8). He had his orders, for God had put them in writing.

Some years ago, I was to take my first lecture tour overseas. I would be sharing the Word in seven countries in Europe and the Middle East for about two months. At that time, I was conference director at The Navigators headquarters at Glen Eyrie in Colorado Springs. We had invited the late Paul Little of Inter-Varsity Christian Fellowship to be our speaker at the Collegiate Conference. During the week that Paul shared the Word with us, I mentioned my forthcoming trip to him, hoping to get some advice. I knew Paul had traveled extensively throughout the world and I was eager to get some counsel from this man of God. I was not disappointed; he gave me some of the best advice I have ever received.

"LeRoy," he said, "when you are ministering overseas, stick with the Bible. The Scriptures teach that God has fashioned all people's hearts alike, and the Word of God speaks to the heart." Paul's words really helped me on that first trip. I should not have been concerned about trying to communicate to such a wide variety of people— Scandinavians, Englishmen, Germans, Dutch, and people of the Middle East. God's Word has universal application.

I have observed the same principle to be true in America. When I spoke to a conference of young men and women in Colorado, for example, a wide variety of people attended—enlisted men from Fort Carson (army), cadets from the Air Force Academy, agricultural science people and engineers from Colorado State University, teachers from Northern Colorado University, and hippie types from the University of Colorado at Boulder. Long hairs, short hairs, no hairs. Disciplined and undisciplined. Levi jackets and beads and uniforms. Spit-polished shoes and sandals. A rainbow of variety.

I stuck with the Bible that conference weekend and people were converted to Christ from every segment. God had fashioned their hearts alike, and the Holy Spirit had used God's Word to speak to those hearts. Philosophically and ideologically, many people in this group were poles apart. Their life-styles screamed at each other. But the message of Jesus Christ from God's Holy Word brought them together into the family of God.

Likewise, whether we seek direction for our homes and families, our businesses or professions, or our personal lives, we must stick with the Bible for every facet of life. And that takes courage.

You might wonder why Joshua's generation of Israelites never turned back, a path which Moses' generation had wanted to do several times during their wilderness wanderings. Basically, it never entered their minds to turn back. This new generation was following God. We too must make that commitment as we live our lives for God. We must never allow thoughts of turning back to find lodging in our minds.

I was pushing weights one day with a young man when he suddenly said, "Man! Sometimes I get so discouraged I think I'll just chuck the whole thing and turn back."

"Back to what?" I asked him.

There is only one way to go, and that's straight ahead. But it takes courage.

THE GRAVE DANGER OF IDOLATRY

Joshua's third challenge warned against idolatry. The main reason the Israelites had been exhorted to stick to the Word of God was "in order that you may not associate with these nations, these which remain among you, or mention the name of their gods, or make anyone swear by them, or serve them, or bow down to them" (Joshua 23:7). God must be first in the lives of His people, and they must have Him as their only foundation (see Luke 6:46-49). Otherwise they are in deep trouble.

Similarly, Paul calls on us as Christians not to be conformed to this world (see Romans 12:2). Someone's life may look great on the outside, but there may be something eating away at his soul—the inner man. That something may be very small, but eventually it will grow. When the storms of life come, Jesus said that in the life of such a person there will be a great fall—the ruin will be visible and great (see Matthew 7:24-27). A firm foundation is a necessity.

If we are to avoid idolatry, we must have in our hearts a great hunger for holiness and a desire to walk with a holy God. And that can come only through the Word of God, for we live in the midst of a hostile environment. We are like deep-sea divers on the bottom of the ocean; everything about us threatens to take our lives. While a deep-sea diver has one thing going for him—his air hose—you and I have a direct line to God. So what if we live in the midst of a hostile environment? Jesus Christ says,

"Surely I will be with you always, to the very end of the age" (Matthew 28:20).

THE CHALLENGE TO CONSISTENCY

The fourth challenge in Joshua's farewell to the people called them to consistency in their walk with God. "You are to cling to the Lord your God, as you have done to this day" (Joshua 23:8). Clinging to the Lord means destroying all things that oppose Him. When I was in charge of The Navigators ministry in the Midwest, I asked that those who were tied in with us memorize a certain Bible verse: "But if you do not drive out the inhabitants of the land from before you, then it shall come about that those whom you let remain of them will become as pricks in your eyes and as thorns in your sides, and they shall trouble you in the land in which you live" (Numbers 33:55).

If we let little sins exist in our lives—sort of mollycoddle this one and put up with that one—our vision for the work of the Lord will be affected. Our forward progress will be impeded, and the sin will become a constant vexation in our lives from that time on. We cannot serve God and pamper little sins. They will get us in trouble, just as the worldly nations got Israel in trouble during the days of the judges.

The same challenge to consistency was echoed in the Early Church: "Now those who had been scattered by the persecution in connection with Stephen traveled as far as Phoenicia, Cyprus and Antioch, telling the message only to Jews. Some of them, however, men from Cyprus and Cyrene, went to Antioch and began to speak to Greeks also, telling them the good news about the Lord Jesus.

The Lord's hand was with them, and a great number of people believed and turned to the Lord. News of this reached the ears of the church at Jerusalem, and they sent Barnabas to Antioch. When he arrived and saw the evidence of the grace of God, he was glad and encouraged them all to remain true to the Lord with all their hearts" (Acts 11:19-23).

How does this passage apply today? It is a challenge for all of us to get into the Word of God for ourselves, to maintain consistency in our prayer lives, and to remain faithful in our fellowship with God and with one another.

THE CALL TO LOVE GOD TOTALLY

The last challenge Joshua gave in his farewell speech was a call for the people of Israel to love the Lord. "Take diligent heed to yourselves to love the Lord your God" (Joshua 23:11). How do we show our love for God? Jesus said, "Whoever has My commands and obeys them, he is the one who loves Me" (John 14:21).

What is the best way that I can generate my love to God? By getting to know Him and committing myself wholly to Him. "You shall love the Lord your God with all your heart and with all your soul and with all your might" (Deuteronomy 6:5). This love is characterized by two things, exclusiveness and intensity. God alone is to be loved, and He is to be loved with everything that we are and have—totally. Jesus later repeated the same commandment in the New Testament (see Matthew 22:35-40).

That's what we are to do—love God totally. That is the first and great commandment. Note again the context of these words: "Love the Lord your God . . . and these words, which I am commanding you today, shall be on your heart" (Deuteronomy 6:5-6). That is the way to spiritual victory.

We are prepared for our battles of life through the Word of God. We must fight our spiritual battles with the Word of God. We must depend on God to give us direction, for the ways God chooses to bring us victory may vary greatly. But the farewell challenge then and now is this: love God, and remember that there is no magic formula for victory.

TOPICS FOR STUDY

1. The faithfulness of God.
2. How to resist temptation (see Matthew 4).
3. How to live courageously in this world.
4. How to avoid twentieth-century idols.
5. The inseparability of obedience and love in the New Testament.
6. The biblical teaching on the Great Commandment—loving God totally.

APPLICATION: What in Joshua's farewell address struck me particularly? How can I specifically apply it in my life?